SPARK YOUR

M○™

THE POWER OF INTEGRATED EFFORT ™

The Ultimate Goal Management System™
Leveraging the Power of Momentum for
Individuals, Businesses, Healthcare, and Academia

JAMES L. ANGLE

Spark Your MO: *The Ultimate Goal Management System*™ - *Leveraging the Power of Momentum for Individuals, Businesses, Healthcare, and Academia*
By James L. Angle
© 2015 Academy for MOmentum

Print ISBN: 978-0-9968229-0-9
eBook ISBN: 978-0-9968229-1-6

Lead Editor: Jennifer Regner
Cover and Interior Design by: Fusion Creative Works, fusioncw.com
Cover Concept and Interior Design Graphic Elements by Felicity Angle

Published by Spark Your MO Publishing

First Printing
Printed in the United States of America

Find more information at academyformomentum.com or call
1-844-MySpark (1-844-697-7275).

This book is dedicated to my loving family
and to all those seeking the answer
to the question, "Now what?"

CONTENTS

CHAPTER ONE

TRANSFORMATION COMES OF AGE

Take a moment and think about your favorite athlete. Then, consider someone else—an actor you admire or a musician whose skill is breathtaking.

One thing that connects them and others who perform at a high level is practice. No matter if it's a golfer looking to add a few yards to his drive or a ballerina preparing for a major performance—deliberate, repetitive, focused practice means everything when striving to do your very best.

Now, imagine the golfer who's never seen a practice range in his entire life, or the dancer who thinks a *pas de deux* is a two-for-one deal at the local bakery. They may know the mechanics of what they need to do, but, for whatever reason, they don't hone that knowledge with practice. The results would be, in their own way, unfortunate. Without a commitment to a carefully constructed practice regimen, no one whose skills or abilities are promising would ever approach mastery.

What's more, anyone of high achievement—be they an athlete or an artist—has an inner drive, a sense of motivation that only they can give themselves. It's a hidden spark that keeps them moving forward, driven by a mindset of powerful momentum.

Most of us have tried to work to improve ourselves in our personal lives, our performance at school, our careers, or our businesses. Unfortunately, not only do many of us lack that spark of momentum that can keep us committed and motivated, but we've lost sight of the importance of ongoing, deliberate practice. We can start off raring to go, but, lacking momentum and an appreciation for practice, our best efforts can fall by the wayside. Or, as I like to put it, we're all left asking the question: "Now what?"

That is the challenge the Academy for MOmentum (AFM) (www.academyformomentum.com) addresses. AFM is an easy to learn, powerful tool to help us practice those skills and behaviors necessary to effect change in our relationships, spirituality, health, finances, careers, and more. This is transformational change we're talking about—genuine and long lasting.

ACADEMY FOR MOMENTUM

HOW I GOT HERE

My name is Jim Angle. Since the beginning of my career I have focused on hospital administration, and for the last nine years have served as a hospital chief executive officer. I majored in sociology as an undergraduate at Rowan University, formerly Glassboro State College, in New Jersey. As a result of my studies, I became intrigued with the socialization of people, families, and civilizations. How do people learn and develop mentally, physically, emotionally, spiritually, and socially throughout their lives? How do groups and civilizations move forward, defining their cultures with every passing year and generation?

Working to obtain my master's degrees (master of social work, Rutgers, The State University of New Jersey; master in health systems administration, Rochester Institute of Technology), I was fortunate to be educated in several areas of critical scientific and theoretical importance: learning and human behavior, clinical social work, organizational change, strategic planning, organizational performance, and leadership. The common thread among these, upon reflection, was that an individual person, a family unit, a group, a team, or an organization all function as a "system." The human body is a functioning system; a family with its various members is a system; a group or team is comprised of people in various roles making up a system; so, too, is an organization a system.

So, to understand, assist, and influence change or transformation, I soon benefited from my education and experience as a "systems thinker." I began my professional career as a mental health program specialist, providing one-on-one teaching and skill development using a psychosocial rehabilitation model of care. It was at that point in time that I became impressed with the ability of some people to effect lasting change when clear and repetitive instruction (the "tell-show-do" teaching method) and support of others are applied consistently over time.

My understanding of people, groups, and organizations began to gel during my career in hospital administration. Observing physicians, clinical providers, and support staff in the vital area of health care, it struck me that the value of deliberate and focused practice—in communicating and working together as a team—was something that few of these very skilled, accomplished people had ever pursued with education or training (let alone had it provided by an organization as a way of doing business routinely). Additionally, organizations continually place demands on the workforce, sometimes without extensive thought and/or understanding of the benefit of the relationship between deliberate practice and performance improvement. I came to learn that the same challenge existed in all sorts of groups, organizations, and businesses (even in our own families). We all recognize the importance of working together, but no resource I came across ever addressed the how-to, purposeful approach to deliberate, repeatable, and consistent practice over time.

My involvement in athletics also underscores the value of practice—and not just in repetition to boost skills. In training to participate in—and successfully complete—the 2002 Lake Placid Ironman triathlon and other endurance events, I came to recognize the power of "integrated effort." By that I mean, the more you work one part of your body, other parts of your body benefit at the same time. For instance, when you practice to improve your bicycling skills, your swimming kick becomes stronger. The cardiovascular benefit from biking and swimming makes running more efficient. Moreover, the discipline of this physical training leads to greater mental sharpness.

Additionally, a sports team, a singer, a band, a speaker, and a runner all have a process and technique to warm up before an event or performance. Knowing that the warm up is important to the performance (expected outcome) of the actual event, the question raised is: "What prevents most people, businesses, and academic institutions from embracing this activity?"

Still, the question remained for me: "Now what?" There were certainly plenty of books available on the advice, education, and importance of developing these sorts of skills, but their usefulness stopped at the last page. There was simply no means—a tool—with which people in all walks of life could benefit from the follow-through of deliberate, repeated, concerted practice to move their lives forward in whatever way they wished.

HOW IT WORKS

That was how AFM came into being. Rather than being just a how-to guide or book, AFM is an interactive and engaging online tool that actively involves participants, both encouraging and challenging them to progress toward whatever goals they deem important—from better communication with family members, to improved personal finance management, to creating a workplace environment where every employee feels valued and involved. AFM can be recognized as the go-to supplemental tool for many of the how-to guides, books, audio and visual mediums, educational courses, online programs, and coaching instructions available to us all. Most of us have heard the term plug-and-play. Now, with AFM, we can activate the term plug-and-practice as we leverage the information and knowledge made available to us.

It's helpful to bear in mind that this is not a passive form of learning—the mere exchange of knowledge. The user takes the goal information he or she wishes to activate and plugs it into the AFM tool. Phrased another way, AFM allows participants to spark their own momentum for change, coupled with the power of thoughtful, integrated effort.

INDIVIDUALS, BUSINESSES, AND ACADEMIC INSTITUTIONS

AFM benefits three related yet distinct groups:

Individuals—People looking for change, growth, or optimal performance, be it in their personal or professional lives.

Businesses—Organizations of all sorts striving for better results, from increased profits to greater employee and customer engagement.

Academic Institutions—Schools at any level searching for strategies to improve their students' performance while better preparing them to meet the challenges and opportunities of an increasingly competitive global environment.

14

ACADEMY FOR MOMENTUM: TEN FACETS

AFM addresses ten vital areas of focus from which program participants can select—a diverse array of facets designed to address the needs of the whole person or whole organization. These are referred to as the ten transformational facets of the AFM service. As an illustration, here are the ten facets geared to individuals, as well as a brief explanation of the role they can play in personal and professional growth (these will be discussed in greater detail in Chapter Three):

- ◇ **Fitness and Recreation**—The value of physical well-being and its effect on other areas of our everyday lives.

- ◇ **Education**—Learning is no longer confined to a traditional classroom. Education can take place in all sorts of venues, from Internet-based distance learning to the intellectual challenges of starting a new job or career. And no one form of learning is less valuable than any other.

- ◇ **Finance**—Effective money management doesn't have to be an exercise in anxiety or the end-all to a happy, fulfilled life. Rather, solid personal finance management involves knowing how to develop a financial plan that's right for you and implementing it consistently.

- ◇ **Relationships**—We all value the ability to get along with and enjoy the company of family members, friends, and professional colleagues. The most effective way to establish and maintain happy and constructive relationships begins with ourselves and how we communicate with others.

✧ **Health**—It's difficult to excel at most any other sort of life skill if you're burdened with poor health. Recognizing and incorporating healthy habits are essential components to support other areas of growth.

✧ **Nutrition**—There's certainly no lack of advice available on what you should eat and what you should avoid. But optimal nutrition involves knowing what works best for you and how to craft an enjoyable and reasonable nutrition plan.

✧ **Work**—Most everyone needs to work to support themselves financially. But work should also be a source of professional and emotional fulfillment rather than a mere paycheck every two weeks.

✧ **Living**—No one lives in an utter vacuum. Being a part of a community or some group at a level you find comfortable is a source of both enjoyment and growth. The same goes for those activities and pastimes that we find both pleasurable and fulfilling.

✧ **Spirituality**—Having a sense of where we all "fit" in the grand scheme of things is an important element of a happy, fulfilled life.

✧ **Harmony**—In many ways, this last area incorporates elements from all prior nine facets. Taken together, harmony can be seen as an ability to be in sync with the people and circumstances at hand. That means a form of constructive acceptance rather than an energy-sapping type of resistance.

ACADEMY FOR MOMENTUM:
INDIVIDUAL FACETS

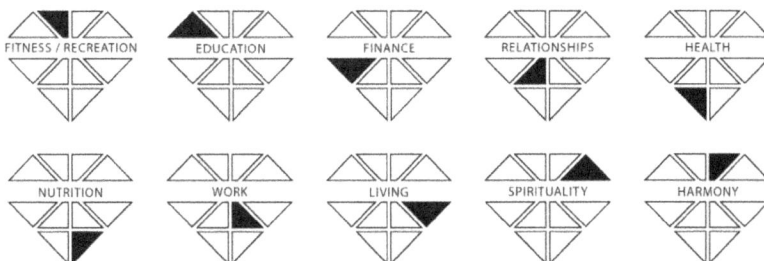

AFM uses the image of a diamond to bring these ten facets together and to help guide participants through the program. It's an appropriate symbol—as facets make up the smooth, defined surface of a diamond, so, too, do AFM's facets come together to drive purposeful, coordinated transformation.

These ten facets don't exist as solitary areas. Given that AFM emphasizes the power of integrated effort, they all function in a highly synergistic fashion. Put another way, when you're working on and growing in one particular facet, you're also improving in other facets—just like the athlete who, in working on her sprinting ability, is also strengthening her long distance biking stamina. Everything interacts with everything else.

THREE MASTERY LEVELS

How do we work and grow in these ten facets? AFM uses a multi-tiered practice model incorporating three ascending, progressive mastery levels. The three mastery levels are:

- ✧ Mastery Level 1: Spark Your MOmentum
- ✧ Mastery Level 2: Practice Rhythm
- ✧ Mastery Level 3: Peak Performance

ACADEMY FOR MOMENTUM:
THREE MASTERY LEVELS

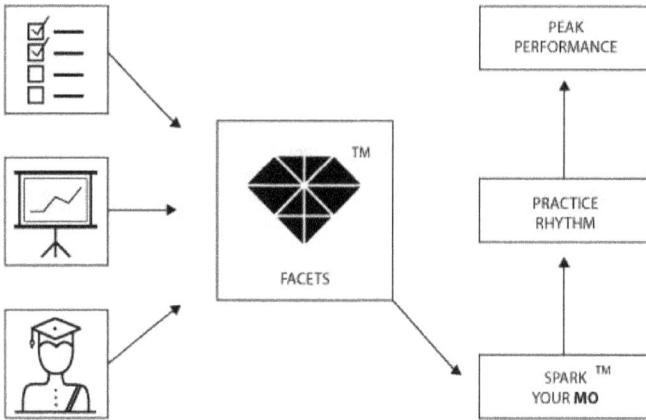

Spark Your MOmentum (or Spark Your MO for short) is the beginning step in the process, designed to get you started in practical, focused forms of practice toward a particular goal. It's intended to get you engaged and motivated!

Here's how it works. First, you select one of the ten facets—let's say health. The system begins with a series of questions designed to gauge where you are now in terms of working on a particular goal and the best way to measure progress. For instance, you'll be asked how often you've thought about improving your health, whether you've developed or followed any particular health improvement regimens, and other questions.

In particular, you'll notice questions that touch on how successful you've been in keeping a health improvement plan going (if you've started one). That is a key component of the overall approach taken by AFM—as the name suggests, getting started is certainly an important step, but maintaining that effort is every bit as critical to achieving lasting, meaningful results. AFM is designed to harness that strong, inner sense of momentum and to build on past successes.

After completing the questions, you then move on to the activities of the first level. This is designed to kick-start your motivation and learning as well as provide practical steps needed to achieve progress (My MO Activation). This is your *why* (why is this important to you, your team, or your organization?).

MASTERY LEVEL 1: SPARK YOUR MO

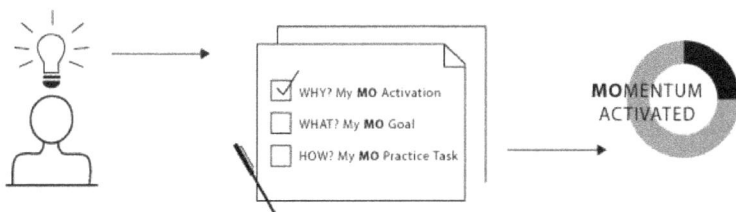

Then you'll be prompted to suggest a particular goal you'd like to achieve—let's say you'd like to eat at least four types of vegetables or fruits every day (My MO Goal). This is your *what*. Having entered that objective into the system, you then set a target date, such as one month from today.

From there, the system moves forward to allow you to add a practice activity (My MO Practice Task). This is your *how*, such as eating a vegetable at each meal. Like the first goal of eating more fruits and vegetables, you enter a due date (defining duration) to complete the goal, in addition to designating a task frequency (e.g., five days per week to begin) and intensity or repetitions (e.g., three times per day). This information is entered into the program.

It's important to point out a few things as we proceed. First, as you enter a new MO practice task and, from there, begin to fulfill the goals you've set for yourself, you'll notice a scoreboard toward the top of the dashboard (the page where all ten facets are displayed). As you complete parts of the task toward your ultimate goal, you'll see that you accumulate points based on your actual completion of steps in AFM and your practice tasks. This is one way to not only measure your progress but also to motivate you further as you continue toward the practice task completion (after all, no matter the game or activity, who doesn't like to rack up a lot of points?). Additionally, the system promotes a form of ownership—as you complete tasks and accumulate points, you feel a part of the process. Your laptop, smart phone, or mobile device allows you to log your completed tasks throughout the day. The program will ask about your preference on when you want to be notified when a task is due (e.g., daily or weekly).

Within the box containing the particular facet you're working on, you'll also notice a small wheel that, with every step toward your goal that's logged into the system, continues to extend and shows you the percentage completed until it makes a complete circle. Once that's done, you've completed that particular mastery level.

From there, the overall system incorporates two additional mastery levels—Practice Rhythm and Peak Performance. These two levels are designed to further the development you began at the Spark Your MO level. At the Practice Rhythm and Peak Performance levels, the tasks become more challenging—their duration and frequency change, as does the intensity with which a particular task is performed.

These two levels also illustrate salient aspects of the overall AFM system. For instance, Practice Rhythm underscores the developmental value of repeated practice—like the golfer who, having learned an optimal swing, repeats the movement hundreds and thousands of times, so, too, does Practice Rhythm encourage repeated actions to move toward mastery of a particular skill or behavior. Further, it cements a sense of habit—just as we all can acquire bad habits simply by doing the same thing over and over, we can also cement positive habits in the same manner (more about the science behind this in the next chapter).

The third level, Peak Performance, is when you really refine and hardwire your skills or behaviors. Peak Performance participants are encouraged to manipulate the duration, intensity, and frequency with which a particular practice task is done and to make any sorts of adjustments that may be applicable to a person or a business. This level can be more time efficient as well, since you can reduce the time (duration) and increase the repetitions (intensity) while still working toward the ultimate mastery level of peak performance. This process of adjusting the duration, frequency, or intensity is what AFM refers to as the "*Speed of MOmentum*" strategy.

ACADEMY FOR MOMENTUM FOR BUSINESSES AND ACADEMIC INSTITUTIONS

The prior section used individuals as the primary example to discuss the system's components and workings. But, as was noted earlier in the chapter, AFM is also geared to serving businesses and academic institutions.

Although the basic theory and function of the program remains the same for these two additional groups, since both of these groups rely on individuals and teams to accomplish work and generate high reliable outcomes (i.e., products or services), there are some differences that are important to point out. For one thing, the transformational facets for businesses and academic institutions are different.

TRANSFORMATIONAL FACETS: BUSINESSES

The transformational facets for businesses, in order, are:

- ✧ Culture of Performance Excellence
- ✧ Operating Performance Results
- ✧ Organizational Development
- ✧ Workforce/Employee Engagement and Experience
- ✧ Customer Engagement and Experience
- ✧ Leadership and Management
- ✧ Communication
- ✧ Planning and Execution
- ✧ Systems Thinking
- ✧ Innovation

ACADEMY FOR MOMENTUM:
BUSINESS FACETS

CULTURE OF PERFORMANCE EXCELLENCE

OPERATING PERFORMANCE RESULTS

ORGANIZATIONAL DEVELOPMENT

WORKFORCE/EMPLOYEE ENGAGEMENT & EXPERIENCE

CUSTOMER ENGAGEMENT & EXPERIENCE

LEADERSHIP & MANAGEMENT

COMMUNICATION

PLANNING & EXECUTION

SYSTEMS THINKING

INNOVATION

TRANSFORMATIONAL FACETS:
ACADEMIC INSTITUTIONS

The transformational facets for academic institutions are:

- ⬦ Culture of Performance Excellence
- ⬦ Research Excellence
- ⬦ Educational Methods—Synchronous
- ⬦ Educational Methods—Asynchronous
- ⬦ Student Engagement and Experience
- ⬦ Schools, Divisions, & Departments Management Leadership
- ⬦ Innovation—Class and Syllabus AFM Value-Add
- ⬦ Instructor, Professor, or Teacher Competency
- ⬦ Communication
- ⬦ Philanthropic Excellence

ACADEMY FOR MOMENTUM:
ACADEMIC INSTITUTIONS FACETS

CULTURE OF PERFORMANCE
EXCELLENCE

RESEARCH EXCELLENCE

EDUCATIONAL METHODS
- SYNCHRONOUS

EDUCATIONAL METHODS
- ASYNCHRONOUS

STUDENT ENGAGEMENT
& EXPERIENCE

SCHOOLS, DIVISION, & DEPARTMENTS
MANAGEMENT LEADERSHIP

INNOVATION - CLASS &
SYLLABUS AFM VALUE-ADD

INSTRUCTOR, PROFESSOR
OR TEACHER COMPETENCY

COMMUNICATION

PHILANTHROPIC EXCELLENCE

You'll note that the facets for these two additional groups differ a good deal from those addressed by the individual program. That's not surprising, given that the goals and objectives of businesses, schools, and other sorts of organizations can differ substantially from those that we, as individuals, might identify. In particular, there's a greater focus on group dynamics—how a number of people work together and interact, and the varied challenges that derive from those larger, more varied, and complex circumstances.

Another unique feature to businesses and organizations is that AFM is designed to meet a group's particular needs or goals. For example, if a business relies on a large, mobile sales force across a large geographic region, the service can be used to place a particular emphasis on a skill or behavior that's expected to be demonstrated by the sales team when interacting with clients and prospects.

But, like programs geared to individuals, the same sort of powerful synergy exists in business and academics. When a group works on one particular goal, they're bound to see improvement in other areas and further overall growth in both personal and profession-al relationships. Moreover, the group also benefits from a strong sense of shared momentum. This can also be described as the *"cause and effect"* MOmentum paradigm. For example, suppose a company has defined a practice task for every salesperson, for every initial customer contact, to explain the benefits of buying a certain product (cause). When all customers are surveyed on whether the salesperson explained the benefits in a meaningful and understandable way, the results will trend in the 90 to100 percent top rating score (effect).

Another example is when a hospital, based on supporting evi-dence, identifies the need to educate its providers as to the best methods for communicating with patients who are anxiety-ridden and experiencing some sort of physical pain (which is to say, most patients). The language-based practice task would be to practice empathic listening, verbal education, and a teach-back response (a healthcare literacy method whereby the practitioner asks the patient to repeat back what they just heard so the practi-tioner can assess clear understanding). This happens during every patient interaction. The result of this practice task is measured in two ways. First, the more proficient the practitioner is in listening and providing education in a way the patient understands, the better the results in the teach-back process on the first or second attempt. The second way to measure the result is to review the patient survey results, which specifically ask about the satisfaction and consistency of provider communication.

WHAT THE ACADEMY FOR MOMENTUM IS NOT

Having offered a brief overview of how AFM works and the varied and powerful benefits it offers, it's useful to point out what the program is not. Simply put, however strong the program's emphasis is on the value of deliberate, repeated, focused practice, nowhere does the program tell you what to practice.

Let's use an example. For instance, if your goal is to lose weight and improve your health, many books and programs go into exhaustive detail about what you should eat and what you should avoid; types of exercises and optimal frequency; and other specific guidelines designed to steer your activities as specifically as possible.

Having just been introduced to the AFM methodology, you can see clearly that the program in no way lays out such prescriptive content. For instance, using the nutrition example, the program doesn't specify how many or what kind of fruits and vegetables you should eat on any given day. Rather, it asks you to set your own goals—how would you like to get started on the path toward better health and nutrition? And, if you think eating more fruits and vegetables is a great place to start, how many would you ideally like to eat? And what kind?

This lack of specific guidelines is in place for a number of reasons. First, how we grow and improve as people are very personal issues. Citing the nutrition example once more, while one person may wish to consume more plant-based food, others may target less fat, salt, or caffeine, and other dietary goals.

Just as important, a central part of an effective learning process is gathering and understanding valuable information that can be vital to whatever growth you wish to achieve. You're not simply handed information and told to use it. Again, that's just an exchange of information—nothing wrong with that, but it doesn't lead to transformational change. Instead, you may do some research to decide what sort of information might serve you best, such as consulting nutrition sources on various ways to lose weight and improve your health (if those are your goals). You choose what information is important to use for growth and plug it into the program to track your progress and improve your performance. Measured practice over time results in transformation.

From there, AFM is designed to use the information you've gathered toward an actionable goal, with specific practice tasks geared toward reaching that goal. That affords program participants a genuine sense of connection with the overall process, as they understand exactly what they're working with and why. And when you're that connected with the process, the probability of success and transformation is that much greater.

HOW DO I SEE IMPROVEMENT?

Given that many books and other forms of self-help options often provide a great deal of information, it's understandable that many people approach any sort of program with a good deal of healthy skepticism. The question is a common one: If I participate in one or more of AFM's facets, how do I know that I'm getting the results I desire? And how soon will all that start to happen?

The AFM system has been carefully designed to allow partici-pants to track progress and growth. As discussed earlier in this chapter, when beginning work on a particular facet, the system asks a series of questions to determine where a user is with regard to their experience. For instance, have you tried to work on this issue before? If so, were you satisfied with the results?

Once a particular level has been completed, the program circles back to ask another series of questions. Here's where you can begin to see results. For example, using the example of the nu-trition facet, you are now answering that, yes, you have a pro-gram in place to eat at least four fruits and vegetables every day. Further, not only have you been able to consistently do so, you can express a sense of satisfaction and achievement in meeting this particular goal.

Pay attention as well to the points you have accumulated during this process. These represent numerical evidence that you have, in fact, put a program into place and are effectively following through on it. You're seeing your progress and success, step by step.

Take note of growth in other areas. For instance, since you're now eating a more healthy diet, your fitness and health facets may also show improvement. Again, this underscores the synergy of AFM's overall design and approach—work on one area or issue, and positive results will become apparent elsewhere. You're wit-nessing the power of integrated effort!

Don't overlook more subjective forms of growth as well. For ex-ample, if you've been working on relationships, are things going more smoothly at home? Is a formerly non-communicative teenager opening up a bit more? At work, does the give-and-take with colleagues seem more productive? Did a sales presentation that once intimidated you to no end seem to go more effectively, with positive feedback and results?

Improvement can be measured in other ways for businesses and schools. Are sales going up? Did a recent customer satisfaction survey show marked improvement in your clients' opinion of your staff and services? At school, have student evaluations of teachers gotten better? Are students enjoying greater success in finding suitable jobs upon graduation?

A common follow-up question on results is how quickly program participants can expect to see these sorts of results. Of course, that can depend on a number of factors—including the person or people taking part in the program, their level of commitment, and other variables—but, as a global yardstick, program participants can expect to see measurable results in as quickly as three months. Even better, the more you continue to work on your goals during the mastery levels, the more substantial and meaningful the results. The AFM program allows you to advance through the mastery levels as many times as you need to, based on your schedule, progress, and ultimate level of performance desired.

To wrap up, AFM works. It's as simple as that. And, to further cement your confidence in the program, the next chapter will offer a brief discussion of the science and research upon which AFM's methodology is built.

CHAPTER TWO

THE SCIENCE BEHIND THE SUCCESS

As I mentioned in the first chapter, many people are a bit skeptical about any program or system that promises wonderful results—justifiably so! Whether it's a form of self-improvement that fails to emphasize deliberate and repeated practice, or a lack of momentum within a particular system or on the part of participants, improving your life in whatever way you deem appropriate has earned the reputation for being a hit-or-miss proposition—at best.

The Academy for MOmentum (AFM) and its programs have been carefully designed to offer you the best possible chances for achieving your goals. The first chapter offered an overview of how the overall program works. In this chapter, we'll look at the science that underscores that system. But not too technically, I promise—just enough to illustrate the solid thinking behind AFM and, in turn, why your confidence will be well rewarded.

TRANSFORMATIONAL DEFINITION AND DRIVERS

Transformational Definition: **A change in the current state of an individual, organization, or academic institution. Change is comprised of what you think, how you feel, and how you act. When a strong influence or stressor is placed on the current state and people engage in the repetitive cycle of thinking, feeling, and acting differently, a transformation has taken place. This transformation results in a new current state.**

NOTE: The current state is always subject to a) change again at any point, or b) holding and solidifying its position through purposeful, deliberate practice around thinking, feeling, and acting behaviors.

That simple definition is useful to bear in mind as we discuss why AFM provides such meaningful results. One reason is that the science behind the AFM program brings together very powerful forces—scientifically-established forces that we can use to bring about positive, lasting change in ourselves as individuals, as well as in organizations and other groups of people. Mezirow & Associates points out that "transformations in habit of mind may be *epochal*, a sudden, dramatic, reorienting insight, or *incremental*, involving a progressive series of transformations in related points of view that culminate in a transformation in habit of mind."

Thus, the first such overriding force consists of the social and behavioral sciences. This, as the name suggests, is the study of how people behave and interact with one another—and, pertinent to our purposes, what sorts of behavior and interaction lead to positive change, and to changes that are less so.

A second is biological science—the study of living things. A third force is the physical sciences—essentially, the study of things that are not living. This would include such disciplines as chemistry and physics.

Putting these three sciences together (triangulation), you can see how they can be used alongside each other to study a whole range of topics. In the case of AFM, they can be applied to understand how we, as humans, develop and transform ourselves—and how we can leverage these sciences to better our lives in whatever ways we wish.

Under the AFM system, these three forces encompass ten powerful "transformational drivers"—sources of enormous import that can not only change us but also bring about significant, long-lasting types of transformation (the kinds that we discussed in the prior chapter). Here are those ten transformational drivers (each has a brief description so you have a general understanding of what that term means without going overboard on the science):

- ◇ Practice, Repetition, and Learning Theories (How practice and repetition improve learning and retention)
- ◇ Cognitive Learning Theory (How and why the brain works as we learn things)
- ◇ The Neuroscience of Habits (What happens in our brains when we practice and acquire habits)

✧ Sociology and Socialization Theory (How we as humans acquire skills and behaviors to function as part of families, groups, and society)

✧ Neuroplasticity Science (How the brain's circuitry changes as a result of behavior, environmental influences, and other factors)

✧ The Law of Angular Momentum (This explains how something is affected by rotation, such as a top that stays upright as it spins)

✧ The Law of Momentum Conservation (The amount of momentum that remains after two things collide)

✧ The Law of Linear Momentum (How an object moves based on its size—or mass—and the velocity with which it is moving)

✧ Gamification Theory (How aspects of game playing, such as accumulating points, can be used in feedback and stimulating behavior change)

✧ Motivational Theory (What motivates us and how influential that effect can be)

All ten of these influences fall under one of the three sciences. For instance, Sociology and Socialization Theory are part of the social and behavioral sciences. By contrast, the momentum-related influences are part of the physical sciences.

ACADEMY FOR MOMENTUM: TRANSFORMATIONAL SCIENTIFIC DRIVERS

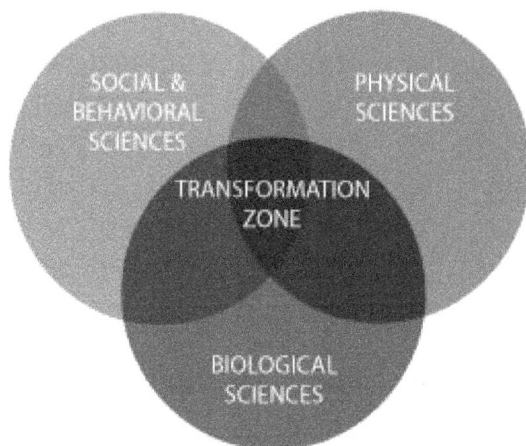

AFM'S TRANSFORMATIONAL FORMULA

This may seem highly technical, but it all ties into a simple, easy-to-understand concept. In fact, the entire process can be summarized in a straightforward formula:

IE + MO + AFM = Transformation

IE (Integrated Effort) + MO (MOmentum) + AFM (Academy for MOmentum) = Transformation

Let's break that down some. IE represents integrated effort. Effort is an observable and repeatable action, like a golfer practicing a swing over and over, or an opera singer who repeatedly runs through scales. Effort derives from our internal willpower to do something or take action. Our willpower derives from informative learning because, as Mezirow & Associates stated, "Learning aimed at increasing our fund of knowledge, at increasing our repertoire of skills, at extending already-established cognitive capacities into new terrain serves the absolutely crucial purpose of deepening the resources available to an existing frame of reference. Such learning is literally in-*form*-ative because it seeks to bring valuable new contents into the existing form of our way of knowing."

FOUR KEY ELEMENTS AND THE POWER OF INTEGRATED EFFORT

Effort also reflects a key difference between the transfer of knowledge and the change that brings about transformation. As we discussed in Chapter One, merely sharing knowledge doesn't necessarily bring about change (like a golf coach explaining the optimal swing to a student). Instead, transformation requires effort (action) that is deliberately practiced and repeated using accurate, focused instruction or guidance. Participation isn't passive.

Since effort is an observable and repeatable action, AFM consists of four key elements:

- ⬥ **Practice Activity**—This is basically the practice itself—the golf swing, the musical scales, the method of communication in an organization
- ⬥ **Practice Duration**—The length of time practice is carried out
- ⬥ **Practice Frequency**—How often practice occurs, i.e., per day, per week, or per month
- ⬥ **Practice Intensity**—The number of repetitions within the identified frequency time frame

MASTERY LEVEL 2: PRACTICE RHYTHM

Deliberate Practice Task Levels

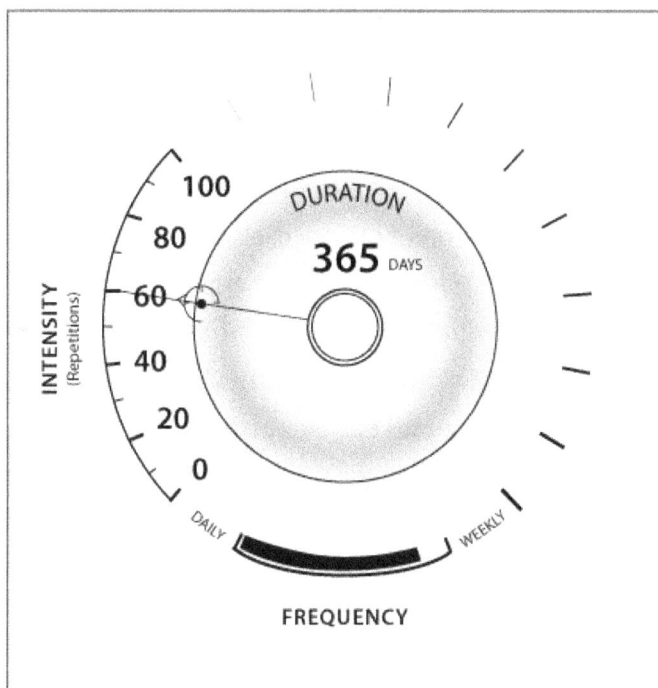

If you think back to the first chapter, we discussed how important (and often overlooked) practice is when it comes to acquiring and perfecting new skills. That not only relates to the simple value of repetition, but to the physical changes that occur in our brains at the same time. Using brain imaging technology, we can see that our brains can modify their structure and function using a process called experience—or learning-dependent plasticity (the capacity for brain structure to physically change—as mentioned in one of the transformational drivers listed above). The neuroscience of habits also supports structural changes in the brain.

But change doesn't happen with mindless repetition. Science has also determined that effective practice that leads to real change must be deliberate, meaningful, motivating, challenging, and rewarding. The AFM system is designed to meet those requirements.

Our transformational formula specifies integrated effort (IE). As we covered in the first chapter, this is a type of effort that has a genuine, pervasive effect. As an example, take the triathlete who, while training to run a great distance, also builds up his strength in swimming and bicycling. Integrated effort also applies to less purely physical activities. For instance, if you work to improve your communication skills at home, they're also bound to improve on the job. It becomes easier and more productive to communicate with coworkers. That means progress occurs on both a personal and professional level with just one form of effort. The effort is integrated across other facets.

ACADEMY FOR MOMENTUM:
THE POWER OF INTEGRATED EFFORT

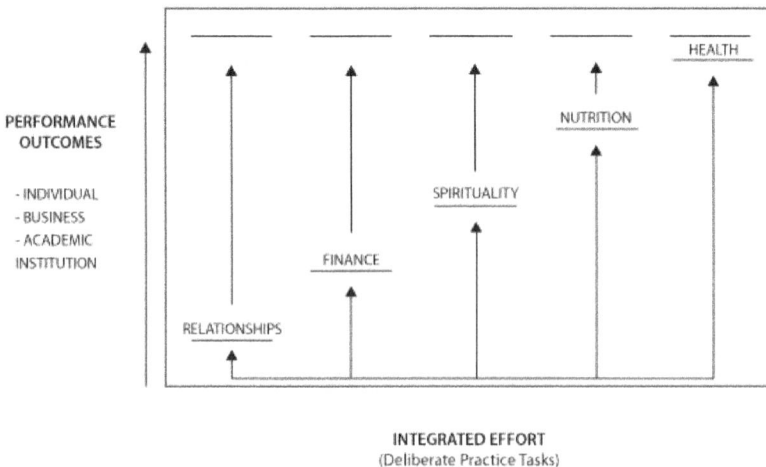

PERFORMANCE
OUTCOMES

- INDIVIDUAL
- BUSINESS
- ACADEMIC
  INSTITUTION

HEALTH

NUTRITION

SPIRITUALITY

FINANCE

RELATIONSHIPS

INTEGRATED EFFORT
(Deliberate Practice Tasks)

In the context of AFM, integrated effort takes the form of a regimen of carefully structured, repeated practice. Citing an example used earlier, choosing to eat four servings of vegetables or fruits every day requires commitment and effort, but once that effort is made, other aspects of our lives benefit—weight loss, better health, greater energy, and other attractive outcomes.

SPEED OF MOMENTUM STRATEGY

MO stands for MOmentum. MOmentum is critical in any sort of pursuit or endeavor—science aside, it's simply the force that keeps things moving forward. Lack of momentum can prove to be a critical missing component when people or organizations look to improve themselves. They may have the knowledge (information) but lack the necessary drive. However committed to a goal someone may be at the outset, an absence of momentum will hinder follow-through, and can make the entire effort frustrating and, ultimately, fruitless. Most of us have heard these sorts of comments where we work: "How do we keep things moving?" or "What prevents us from reaching our goals?" or "Is this the next 'flavor of the month'?" or "Our results have been flat for a long time."

AFM doesn't allow that to happen. With three ascending mastery levels, the program is specifically geared to activate, accelerate, and sustain momentum:

 ✧ **Level One**—Spark Your MO: By researching and selecting a goal, your choice to actively pursue some sort of goal represents the initial force of momentum—a powerful kick-start to the process.

✧ **Level Two**—Practice Rhythm: Here, the science of habit comes into play. Simply put, the more you deliberately practice something, the more you improve while cementing a habit. Momentum also continues to build and accelerate.

✧ **Level Three**—Peak Performance: Increasing momentum and increasing improvement culminate in actions, becoming highly reliable, and sustaining your transformational state.

ACADEMY FOR MOMENTUM: 3 MASTERY LEVELS

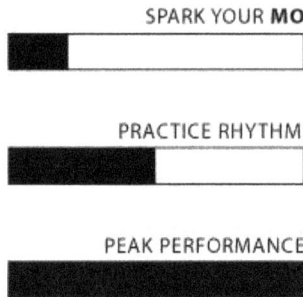

SPARK YOUR **MO**

PRACTICE RHYTHM

PEAK PERFORMANCE

In the context of our formula, MO is the energy of effort combined with use of the AFM tool. Whoever is using the AFM system—be it a person, organization, or academic institution—effectively has MOmentum. Once MOmentum is sparked and sustained at the higher levels of the AFM system, a greater source of energy is necessary to reduce or stop it. We can see a parallel here with the Law of Linear Momentum in the example of a moving truck. That truck, weighing five tons and travelling at 80 mph, will require a greater source of energy to stop than if that truck was travelling at ten mph. In the same way, when 80 people at a business or academic institution are focused on the same goal and practicing an activity consistently, there would need to be a greater source of energy to stop it. The MOmentum builds.

Factors in an organization that might slow MOmentum include:

◇ All members are not practicing (consistency), or their deliberate practice tasks are not completed accurately (quality).

◇ There is no tool to ensure consistency (accountability).

◇ Team members were not actively involved in the goal-setting process and practice activity plan. As a result, they lack "buy-in" (engagement).

◇ Staff and leader changes create a situation where a "new way" seems better (commitment).

The Speed of MOmentum strategy can also come into play. This refers to changes in practice duration, frequency, and intensity (repetitions) that can be used to meet a specific goal within a certain amount of time. For instance, based on customer feedback and other barometers, a restaurant business may need to improve the communication skills of employees who come into contact with the public, such as reception personnel and wait staff. Moreover, since the restaurant business is extremely competitive, management wants to see positive results in just three months. By adjusting AFM practice duration, frequency, and intensity, by the end of three months, restaurant personnel are more confident and competent when greeting, explaining wait times, and talking with customers. That underscores AFM's capacity to adjust to meet whatever goals and time frames are necessary.

MASTERY LEVEL 3 : PEAK PERFORMANCE

Deliberate Practice Task Levels

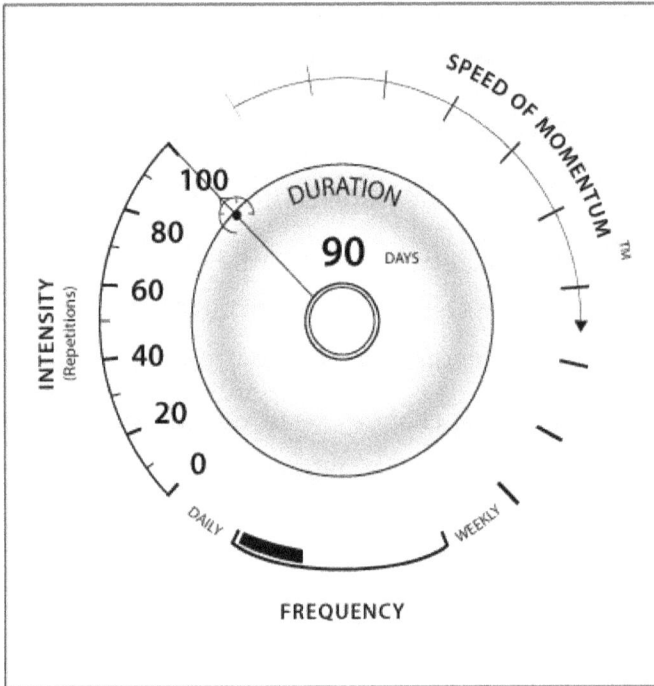

AFM is the third and final element in the equation. This is the overall program that brings integrated effort and momentum together, providing structure, an easy-to-understand means of tracking progress, and a means of maintaining and increasing momentum. The physical sciences tell us that everything remains at rest until it connects with an external force—in this case, AFM.

The result—as represented by the end product of our simple formula—is genuine, meaningful, and long-lasting transformation.

Progress is easy to measure. By receiving points and other barometers that highlight progress (here, gamification theory comes in), program participants know they're moving in the right direction—a sense of fulfillment and achievement that further strengthens overall momentum and commitment. Science refers to this as "reinforcement contingencies"—do something and you're rewarded accordingly. The more you repeat this particular action and the more you're rewarded, the more firmly implanted (and more automatic) the practice becomes. You've transformed yourself!

To make certain that the practice of AFM remains challenging, interesting, and rewarding, the program also offers a journal section. This allows users the chance to record results, observations, and other thoughts as they progress through AFM. The journaling feature lets participants note both positive and challenging experiences as well as ideas that may prove useful in future goal activity. (The journaling feature is entirely secure, so users need not worry about others reading their thoughts and feedback.)

I've witnessed firsthand how these factors and practices can produce real and positive change. I have experience overseeing a workforce of about 3,000 people and, as an overall group, as well as in individual departments and services, we all were constantly working to become better at our jobs and to improve communication amongst ourselves, and with patients and families. And, once we established our clear goals and why those goals mattered, and executed on deliberate practice tasks, momentum was activated. The power of that momentum and focus became absolutely crystal clear. And once hundreds of people were actively practicing, only a more powerful force could bring it to a halt—it was virtually impossible to stop. Even one person who was determined not to cooperate was powerless to halt the momentum. It was a force to be reckoned with!

There's more at play here than just momentum; integrated effort is also at work. One task or participant's contribution works together with the contributions of others to produce something bigger. The whole is greater than the sum of the parts. Just as one member of a symphony orchestra who works to improve his skills can benefit those who are also in his section, so, too, can employees, determined to do what they can to reach a certain goal, boost the effort and commitment of those around them.

This all underscores the overriding holistic nature of the AFM program. Put simply, everything is designed to work in conjunction with everything else, from integrated effort, to increasing momentum, to more deliberate and focused practice that results in transformational results.

The science behind AFM also discredits the assumption that improvement and growth are chance pursuits—goals that only a select, fortunate few can attain. AFM not only puts those desirable results within the reach of us, but does so systematically, measurably, and with outcomes that are both transformative and long-lasting.

ACADEMY FOR MOMENTUM:
MASTERY LEVELS STRATEGY

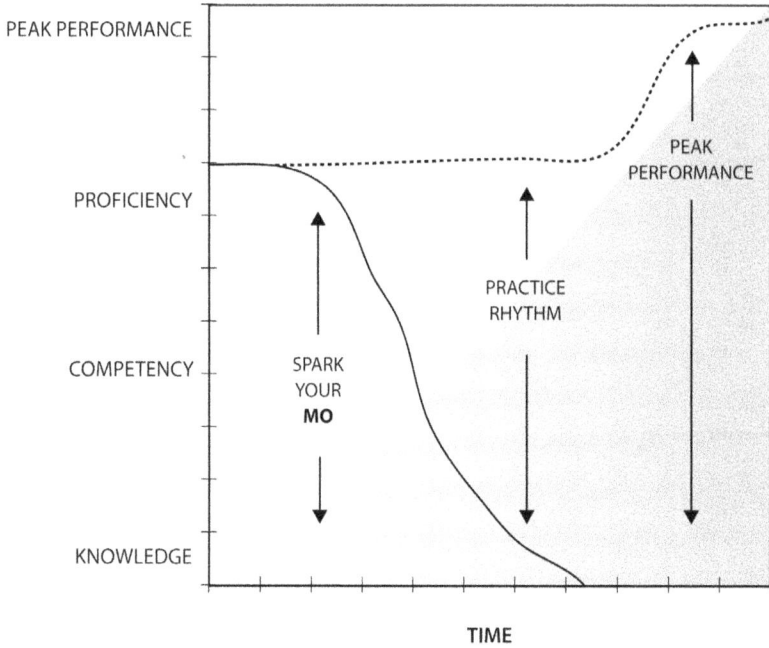

Performance over time **without** ongoing deliberate, purposeful, focused practice.

Performance over time **with** ongoing deliberate, purposeful, focused practice.

Transformational Zone

CHAPTER THREE

TRANSFORMATION, ONE PERSON AT A TIME

An old saying has it that every journey begins with a single step. For people looking to improve their lives—toward whatever goals they deem valuable and appropriate—that single step can be the Academy for MOmentum's (AFM) program for individual users.

It makes sense to refer to the individual program as a suitable jumping-off point. For many, it's natural to look to yourself first when considering aspects of your life that you'd like to improve or enjoy more. Moreover, even if your goals include group-focused relationships—better communication at work or more lively classroom discussions—it makes sense to begin with something over which you have complete, utter control. And that's you.

FACETS AND LIFE CYCLES

The ten individual program facets were listed back in Chapter One. For the sake of convenience, here they are again:

◇ Fitness and Recreation

◇ Education

✧ Finance

✧ Relationships

✧ Health

✧ Nutrition

✧ Work

✧ Living

✧ Spirituality

✧ Harmony

The ten facets have been designed to address a broad array of issues and challenges that we all face in our lives. Just how important one facet happens to be will depend on the individual—for instance, with finance, some users may welcome this tool as a way to put a family budget into place, start saving for a child's college education, or other financial goals. Others may feel their personal finances are in pretty good shape—as a result, other facets may hold greater interest.

Despite these differences, the ten individual facets together make up what I refer to as a personal life cycle. By that, I mean most people will encounter all ten of these issues at some point in their lives. Their importance and value may differ depending on where someone happens to be at a particular juncture in their experiences but, taken as a whole, chances are we all will come across these issues.

That's one reason why the facets are in no particular order. To reinforce a central point, AFM emphasizes the specifics of an individual. Since one facet may be of more immediate importance to one person than it might be to another, the program doesn't offer any sort of recommendation as to which facet a user should work with. That's entirely up to them.

So, too, is the goal associated with a particular facet completely up to the user's choice. Referring once more to the finance facet, one person may wish to work on reducing credit card debt; another may want to get a retirement funding program in place. That—and the research and legwork necessary to know what precisely goes into pursuit of a particular goal—is utterly up to them. That makes participation active, engaging, and, in the end, more fun and rewarding.

Age and other aspects of personal circumstances can also have an effect on which facet appeals to any one user. For instance, someone who's 25 and single may be particularly drawn to certain facets, such as health or nutrition. By the time that person is 40 or so, he may be married with two children. That can impact which facet may be of greater interest then—college savings, paying down a mortgage, moving up in, or perhaps changing, a career. Even the same facet may be framed in an entirely different light—while a 25-year-old may strive to run a marathon every two months, that same individual fifteen or twenty years down the line may be happy with a 10K when opportunity and time for sufficient training permit.

That circles back to the concept of the life cycle of the ten facets. As we move through our lives, our priorities, goals, and dreams change. The AFM is geared to coming along for the entire journey.

ACADEMY FOR MOMENTUM:
INDIVIDUAL LIFE CYCLE

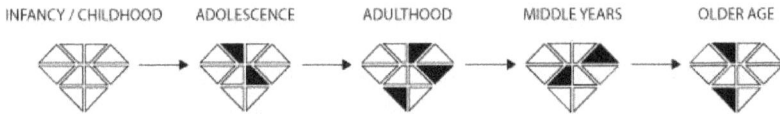

INFANCY / CHILDHOOD   ADOLESCENCE   ADULTHOOD   MIDDLE YEARS   OLDER AGE

"YOU'VE GOT TO BE KIDDING ME!"

Any form of self-improvement can be met with a measure of skepticism, if not outright disbelief. As I touched on earlier, that may be caused by disappointment from prior attempts to: lose weight, earn a promotion at work, or almost any other sort of unfulfilled goal.

In other cases, a particular goal may seem so far-fetched that any effort to pursue it would feel like a complete waste of time and energy. Skepticism doesn't necessarily derive from past experience—here, a goal, however attractive, simply seems completely out of reach from the get-go.

For the moment, let's use a stereotype to discuss how AFM can help with this particular situation. A 40-something man, twenty pounds overweight, sedentary, and far fonder of beer and pretzels than broccoli and papaya, nonetheless knows that his lifestyle may have serious consequences in the future.

But exercise? And a sensible diet?

"Are you kidding me?" he blusters. "I've seen all those infomercials on television, where all those buff models do one-handed pushups! I can barely get off the couch! And, besides, I wouldn't have the foggiest idea where to begin! Tofu burgers? Not likely!"

TRANSFORMATION, ONE PERSON AT A TIME

It's true enough that our friend isn't exactly poised to scale El Capitan in a few weeks' time—or, for that matter, capture first prize at the soy chili cook-off at the local natural foods store. But, he is capable of taking a walk around the block once a day and learning to cook brown rice instead of white. All he needs is to be reminded of those sorts of more realistic possibilities.

AFM addresses that very real need. For one thing, the program is as focused on our exercise-challenged friend as it is on an experienced weightlifter. The secret is in the starting point, which is entirely up to the individual. An out-of-shape person may find a half-mile stroll around the high school track both challenging and invigorating, while a 10K veteran may be more focused on shaving a few seconds off her personal best. A devoted vegan may decide to make his own plant-based cheese; the couch potato and TV clicker may decide low-fat chips are a reasonable way to begin improving his health.

The important idea is that getting started can be half the battle. By having the individual decide what's best for him—and, in so doing, perform some legwork to understand the opportunity and potential hurdles to that decision—the choice to improve is naturally engaging and appropriate. Improvement no longer seems as absurdly out of reach as it once might have been—it's just more reasonable and attainable.

That advantage carries over as individuals progress toward their goals. Proceeding through the challenges of the three mastery levels of practice, a user can decide how to ramp up their activities—and, in so doing, maintain and build the kind of momentum that's critical to lasting success.

Another plus to the AFM online service is that it's always there at the ready. The AFM system recognizes the fact that only you know when you're ready to take something on—and at what level.

That flexibility also applies to changing circumstances. For instance, what if our couch-shackled friend met a perfectly lovely, charming woman—a woman who happened to be an accomplished distance swimmer? He may not be able to match her swimming abilities right off the bat, but he can certainly set and fulfill the goal of five laps in the pool three times a week so they have more in common. (Even the most accomplished athlete knows that everyone has to start somewhere.) By the same token, perhaps someone realizes that, after a few years, her career growth is stumbling—while it may have never occurred to her before, it might seem high time to get an advanced degree online. Again, AFM is there to address whatever issue or opportunity someone decides warrants attention.

"I WONDER WHAT ELSE I CAN DO?"

It's already been established that there's no preset order that users need to follow when using AFM's individual goal tool. That leads us to another understandable question: How many facets should I take on at once?

It may come as a shock (sarcasm intended), but that's an entirely personal issue. For some users, particularly those making their way through the program for the first time, one facet at a time might seem sufficiently challenging. Other users may not feel they're doing all they possibly can unless they have several facets underway at the same time.

Again, it's up to you. AFM allows you to choose the specifics of your goal, crafted to your particular needs and objectives. And whether that happens by itself or in concert with other facets is entirely your call.

Bear in mind, though, that synergy and integrated effort are at the heart of the AFM system, as nothing occurs completely in a vacuum. As we've discussed before, improvement in one area of your life is bound to positively impact other areas, whether that was your intent or not.

That can also come into play with regard to the number of goals you choose to pursue. As you work on one particular goal and begin to experience positive results, it's only natural to begin to wonder: "What else can I do?" For instance, someone who is working on debt reduction—and doing so successfully—may become curious about what else could be done with all that money saved. Retirement? An addition to the house? Next thing you know, you've got another functioning facet under your belt, thanks to the innate synergy of the program.

The bottom line is that, when it comes to individual goals and self-improvement, the AFM program offers a flexible, personal system that's designed to produce meaningful transformation. What you want to transform is entirely your decision—AFM is ready to help you move toward that goal (or goals) in a systematic, fun, and measurable way.

CHAPTER FOUR

THE POWER OF GROUP TRANSFORMATION

Referring to the dynamics of a group, Henry Ford once remarked: "Coming together is a beginning; keeping together is progress; working together is success."

Although the specifics have certainly changed since Ford's time, companies and other groups today have to cope with a different, but no less imposing, environment. Workers routinely change jobs—and even careers—many times throughout their working lives. Unlike Ford's assembly line workers, employees today have a greater and more varied involvement in their company's activities, culture, and values. Moreover, for many companies and organizations, their "place of business" is truly global—an imposing diversity of peoples and societies. Those and other factors require continual adjustment and adaptation.

Still, the essential task of a group trying to come together to achieve shared goals and objectives hasn't changed at all. That's the challenge that the Academy for MOmentum's (AFM) group program is designed to address, putting genuine and compelling group transformation within reach, no matter if it's a sports team comprised of a dozen players or a company with tens of thousands of employees with varied experience and cultural backgrounds.

PEOPLE, NOT "THINGS"

AFM approaches the task of group transformation from the perspective that any group, regardless of size, is comprised of individual people—the very same sort of people who can pursue transformative change on their own through AFM's individual program.

That raises a singular issue particular to group change. As we've discussed, many people have tried to transform central elements of their lives, only to end up disappointed and discouraged. With just one person, that experience is limited and, in a sense, confined.

That sense of frustration can be magnified many times over in a group setting, making the challenge of constructive change all the more difficult. Look at it this way: one person trying unsuccessfully to lose weight can keep his or her frustration to him- or herself. A group of 1,000 employees individually trying to inspire management to consider an on-site workout facility—without a concerted, measurable plan—only to be repeatedly rebuffed, can raise that sort of frustration to a higher level—shared by more, talked about by more, and, ultimately, creating a greater obstacle that can spread and become that much more difficult to overcome.

The AFM program is designed to address that issue before it grows into a genuine problem (or missed opportunity). By focusing on individuals as parts that comprise a whole, the program, when used by a group—rather than on an abstract company or organization that exists completely separate from its individual parts—is able to leverage the same sorts of powerful, positive forces that exist on an individual basis: the value of goal-focused practice, repetition, increasing level of challenge, and, in particular, momentum.

THE SCIENCE OF GROUP MOMENTUM

Anyone who's tried to introduce and successfully oversee—not to mention participate in—significant change within a group of people knows all too well the obstacles that such a situation presents. One of the most immediate and obvious issues is that, rather than one person deciding to pursue a particular goal, you're effectively trying to get many people to make that same sort of decision—to buy into the idea that the objective is worth achieving and, from there, to move forward as a group in a systematic and constructive manner.

AFM leverages scientific law to make this process both effective and measurable. Think back to our discussion about the basic formula that underlies the program: IE (Integrated Effort) plus MO (MOmentum), plus the tool of AFM, results in Transformation.

The AFM program emphasizes the essential value and import of integrated effort—effort that is carefully directed and managed through the program's increasing levels of practice and mastery. Remember, too, that the effort is integrated—as your skills grow in one area, you'll also see improvement elsewhere.

This is particularly powerful in a group setting. Let's say a 50-person department in a company is charged with trimming operating expenses by five percent over the next six months. As a group, they decide to limit the use of paper and other tangible expenses as much as possible. They set their first practice level by trying to use ten fewer paper products per person per week. Just the numbers alone—50 people times ten pieces of paper—would suggest this is a very effective starting point in holding down costs.

But other benefits become apparent at the same time. For instance, since less paper is being used, so, too, are costs for pens, printing cartridges, and other associated expenses going down. Additionally, some employees find that their word processing skills are improving, given that they need to make certain a document is in the best shape possible before it's printed.

But what's particularly important in our formula is the role of momentum. Here, a simple example is helpful: Think about the last time you were in a crowd of people. Suddenly, the group begins to move in a particular direction. Try as you might to go in an opposite direction, you're nevertheless "swept up" and carried by the group. The faster the group moves, the faster you move along as well. This is the law of linear momentum—the greater the mass of an object in motion, the greater its momentum.

That illustrates the value of momentum in a group setting. Using the same parameters, one person practicing and making progress toward a particular goal has a certain amount of momentum. But a group, given its greater size, has that much more momentum, not to mention synergy. The group intensifies individual and group progress. Not only can that lead to greater increases in momentum, it also makes the group's forward progress that much harder to stop. Even if some people in the group are less than wholly enthusiastic about a particular goal, the dynamics of group momentum help ensure positive progress.

Another central feature of the AFM system limits the influence that a group member's lack of enthusiasm or unwillingness to buy into group objectives can have. That's because group members are responsible for choosing a suitable goal as well as the means with which to attain it. In some cases, groups choose the same goal and means: "Let's all work to cut operating expenses five percent by using less paper." In other instances, the goal can be pursued by different means: "Jerry's department will work to cut costs by using less paper. Jennifer's team will be charged with making certain that all equipment not in use is turned off and unplugged."

It's important to remember the inherent individuality of the AFM system, even when it's being used in a group setting. Although the goal in question may be one of several in a group focus (the five percent reduction in operating costs), each person within the group is responsible for maintaining and recording their own practice task and participation. For some, that may mean using less paper, while others make certain all the lights are out after five p.m. The AFM system incorporates all those forms of individual participation and practice which, in turn, are measured in the larger framework of group progress.

This approach also lets all participants feel a genuine connection to both the goal and the ways in which they are pursuing it. There's a sense of a team dynamic, of wanting to do your best so that the entire group benefits. That can boost effort which, in turn, increases momentum—and, ultimately, progress toward a desired goal.

ACADEMY FOR MOMENTUM:
ALIGNED INTEGRATED EFFORT SCENARIOS
BUSINESS & ACADEMIC INSTITUTIONS

 **SCENARIO 1**

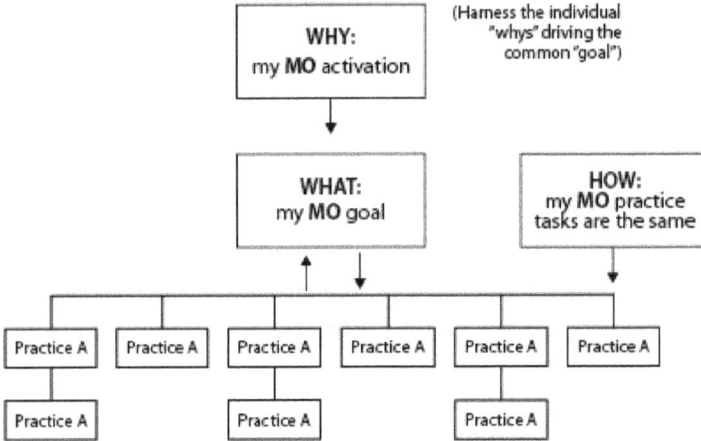

WHY:
my **MO** activation

(Harness the individual "whys" driving the common "goal")

WHAT:
my **MO** goal

HOW:
my **MO** practice tasks are the same

| Practice A | Practice A | Practice A | Practice A | Practice A | Practice A |

| Practice A | | Practice A | | Practice A | |

 **SCENARIO 2**

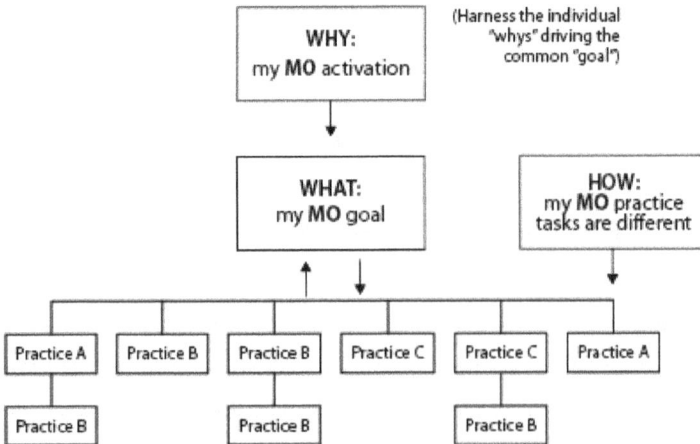

WHY:
my **MO** activation

(Harness the individual "whys" driving the common "goal")

WHAT:
my **MO** goal

HOW:
my **MO** practice tasks are different

| Practice A | Practice B | Practice B | Practice C | Practice C | Practice A |

| Practice B | | Practice B | | Practice B | |

(Practice tasks are different based on the organization's attributes, culture, performance, location, customer requirements, etc.)

INHERENT FLEXIBILITY

Like the program geared to individuals, the AFM organizational program starts with ten suggested facets with which organizations of all sorts can bring about effective transformation:

- ◇ Culture of Performance Excellence
- ◇ Operating Performance Results
- ◇ Organizational Development
- ◇ Workforce/Employee Engagement and Experience
- ◇ Customer Engagement and Experience
- ◇ Leadership and Management
- ◇ Communication
- ◇ Planning and Execution
- ◇ Systems Thinking
- ◇ Innovation

These ten facets offer a broad range of interpretation and use within the AFM system. For instance, operating performance results may mean higher profits for one organization; for another, improved quality or safety might be the benchmarks. Again, AFM allows each group or organization to choose those sorts of specific goals that matter most to them, as well as forms of deliberate practice and repetition best suited to attaining those objectives.

The AFM group system also allows groups and organizations to customize various elements of the program. For instance, certain facets may be particularly important to one organization, but less so for another. Accordingly, the AFM model allows groups to practice and progress in those facets that best benefit their goals and objectives.

AFM also accommodates the broad range of time frames within which most organizations must operate. For instance, a sales company beginning a new fiscal year hopes to increase profits by the end of the second quarter. To meet this goal, the company decides on a customer engagement program to better salespersons' relationships with clients. With an eye on results due by the end of the second quarter, their AFM practice program is particularly rigorous in frequency and intensity—salespeople target the end of the first quarter to complete AFM's Peak Performance Level so sales results can begin to accrue in the following three months.

The effort pays off handsomely. Second quarter sales results are at company-level records—thanks in large part to the company's decision to craft their particular AFM practice to a short, aggressive time frame.

Like the individual program, the AFM group system isn't focused exclusively on correcting problems and perceived shortfalls (such as lagging sales). AFM group participants are also encouraged to identify and pursue goals and objectives proactively. Have a look at the suggested organization questions in the appendix—not all of them focus on repairing a problem. Rather, they also allow groups to recognize what they're particularly good at and work to improve even further—or to consider a goal that they've never pursued or even considered before.

THE POWER OF GROUP TRANSFORMATION

Businesses, organizations, and other types of groups exist to achieve positive results. To do that, they must remain flexible and responsive to a constantly changing set of challenges and circumstances. The AFM system puts a powerful tool in their hands to offer a systematic and measurable means to achieve genuine transformation to meet those needs.

CHAPTER FIVE

AFM GOES TO SCHOOL

Even the most disconnected student knows what school is supposed to be about—you sit there for a certain number of hours every day and you listen to things you will be expected to know.

Granted, a high-achieving student certainly views school with a greater sense of commitment—in terms of growing as a person or acquiring knowledge that will be useful in a career—but the basic formula remains the same. Teachers offer knowledge, students receive that knowledge.

Unfortunately, there's a great deal of value lost in that simple equation. True, students may learn, but are they able to leverage that knowledge to its utmost potential? And, taking that question to a broader platform, how can that knowledge be put to most effective use once their academic days are done and their working lives begin? To quote Mezirow once again: " . . . learning aimed at changes not only in *what* we know but changes in *how* we know has an almost opposite rhythm about it and comes closer to the etymological meaning of *education* ('leading out').

'Informative learning' involves a kind of leading in, or completing of the form. Trans-*form*-ative learning puts the form itself at risk of change (and not just change but increased capacity)."

The Academy for MOmentum's (AFM) academically-geared service is designed to address those and other issues. As it does with individuals, companies, and other groups, AFM can bring genuine transformative change to both students and teachers, helping to build an academic model that is more engaging, efficient, and focused on preparing students for the highest level of achievement possible in whatever pursuits they may choose to follow.

LEARNING PUT INTO PRACTICE

The core feature of the AFM program is a regimen of steadily increasing practice levels designed to improve skills on both the individual and group level. That's easy to see with individuals and customers—a person may wish to lose weight and get into better shape while a company may target increased sales or better customer retention.

The AFM program for academic institutions shares many of those sorts of goals but also emphasizes the pragmatic application of what students learn in a classroom setting. For instance, a high school student may spend weeks studying the civil rights movement of the 1950s and 1960s, reading about the struggle African Americans encountered in all sorts of situations, such as securing a reliable means of voting.

In a conventional school setting, that "lesson" may stop at the end of the textbook chapter on the civil rights movement.

AFM doesn't allow for that sort of abrupt and unfulfilling conclusion. Rather, the program encourages students to "practice" what they've learned to gain a more complete understanding of the historic circumstances and challenges—and, in so doing, become more fully engaged with all aspects of the subject.

How might that happen? One level of practice of AFM for history students might be a project of voter registration—over the next month, helping fifteen people in the community register to vote. In that sense, the process of obtaining the right to vote doesn't remain in the abstract domain of a textbook. Instead, students learn first-hand of the challenges inherent in that situation—not merely the history and mechanics of voter registration itself. The activity of registering voters, especially those who are African American, makes real the struggle to obtain the right to vote. It operationalizes the learning.

That also illustrates the value of integrated effort that's part of every aspect of the AFM program. As a student canvasses a neighborhood looking to register voters, a student's communication skills also improve as he interacts with all sorts of different people. Likewise, research skills may also benefit as the student canvasser needs to be aware of the pressing issues faced by the community in order for prospective voters to recognize the importance of voting.

Integrated effort and the growing momentum of the AFM program can also drive students to further levels of experience. For instance, a student finding a community that's apathetic about public affairs through his voter registration efforts may discover an interest in running for office to improve community engagement. That would lead to the enhancement of other skills, such as public speaking, fundraising, marketing, and public outreach.

These and other examples illustrate AFM's capacity to take classroom learning and elevate it into pragmatic, beneficial experience—not to mention broadening the overall learning experience by fostering improvement in other skills and abilities. By tracking primary goal efforts, additional goal achievement is seen. The momentum initiated with one goal carries over to some of the other goals, making them easier to attain and leading to greater overall progress.

NOT JUST BETTER STUDENTS, BETTER SCHOOLS

Like any organization, schools constantly strive to operate more efficiently and produce better results. In that sense, a school can seem much like a business—only in this setting, it's the students who are the "customers" seeking top notch service. And AFM is every bit as pragmatic in helping academic institutions of all sorts provide a superior learning environment.

Like any business or organization, a school can be hindered by conflicting forces—varied departments vying for valuable funding or faculty and staff members who have differing viewpoints on how best to serve their students. In this regard, AFM can be seen as a galvanizing tool. Using the system much as a group in a business or other organization would, school staff can leverage the AFM system to work together to identify common goals and objectives, while minimizing differences and any inherent "politics"—not to mention objectively assessing student progress, a hotly debated subject for many years.

For example, let's say a preparatory school wants to better prepare their students for the college admission process by improving SAT scores. Rather than a splintering of viewpoints and ideas—one segment of the faculty believes specific instruction in math should be emphasized, while others favor a more rigorous language-based approach—AFM brings all concerned parties together to focus on shared, integrated effort. In this case, math faculty agree to focus on improving language-based math skills, while the English department sets out to focus on inductive and deductive reasoning, skills that are used to solve math problems as well as to shape written compositions. The coordinated efforts of the two seemingly distinct departments enhance the overall skills tested in the SAT.

As is the case in a corporate setting, individual faculty and staff members are charged with focused practice and carefully tracking results in their AFM program. The tracking and the progression toward goal attainment that the program offers give faculty more immediate proof of their efforts, rather than waiting for SAT scores to come out, not to mention relying solely on a test score to demonstrate skill advancement.

Other areas of the overall academic experience can also benefit with the use of AFM. For instance, an instructor whose knowledge of his or her topic is encyclopedic but who struggles to communicate with students may use the program to practice and improve on instructive forms of interaction.

Students can also use the program to become, in effect, better students, and not just from the standpoint of grades or similar markers of academic achievement. By integrating and operationalizing their knowledge, they can measure their own progress. They don't need to rely on an oftentimes subjective grading system, but can see their progress by using the AFM tool.

As an example, say a student finds elements of a particular lecture confusing. Rather than merely trying to cope with the situation as best as possible or stopping in to see the professor, a student can use AFM to outline where he is confused, what questions to ask the professor, and how to practice the suggestions the professor offers. The student can then leverage this improved understanding to help master the difficult material. If the student and the professor tracked his progress together, there might very well be improved lecture techniques on the professor's part as well. Maybe there was an area not explained well enough for initial understanding by several students. The benefit becomes synergistic. The student's enhanced understanding leads to the professor's improved lecture skills.

FLEXIBLE BY DESIGN

As is the case with individual—and group-focused programs—the AFM academic system offers ten transformational facets which can be directed toward a variety of areas ripe for change:

- ✧ Culture of Performance Excellence
- ✧ Research Excellence
- ✧ Educational Methods—Synchronous

⬦ Educational Methods—Asynchronous

⬦ Student Engagement and Experience

⬦ Schools, Divisions, and Departments Management Leadership

⬦ Innovation—Class and Syllabus AFM Value-Add

⬦ Instructor, Professor, or Teacher Competency

⬦ Communication

⬦ Philanthropic Excellence

Consistent with other elements of the overall AFM program, these ten facets have been designed with a good deal of flexibility in mind. The pre-established facets can be modified to meet each institution's need.

BETTER STUDENTS, BETTER GRADUATES

In the end, AFM is built to allow program participants to achieve results by the continual monitoring of efforts. The potential benefit to academic institutions is huge: students graduate with the ability to self-monitor and motivate and to make needed adjustments along the way. They measure where they are, where they want to be, and how to get there, and practice the skills needed to move forward with their lives via the AFM tool. They emerge from college not just learners, but doers. They have operationalized their knowledge rather than just regurgitating facts on tests or laboring at internships.

These improved skills are not limited to the four walls of the classroom—teachers who are better communicators and students who are more active and involved make for a richer, more productive society. There is greater integration of efforts and outcomes.

This brings us back to the question of preparation—how well are schools helping students prepare to apply the knowledge they've acquired? AFM's focus on the pragmatic addresses this directly by encouraging and measuring real-world forms of practice and skill improvement.

Think back to the history student who, having graduated, wants to be hired by a political action committee geared to boosting voter turnout. Many students' résumés might be limited to classroom study of the topic, but the student who also participated in AFM will be able to cite practical experience—neighborhood canvassing, number of voters registered, common registration challenges, or a grasp of community issues. Add to that other benefits derived from integrated effort—improved written and communication skills, organizational ability, to cite a few—and the end product is a superior job candidate poised to contribute and excel.

Students aren't the only ones to benefit from a superior education and improved career prospects. Academic institutions of all sorts are constantly focused on criteria necessary to maintain suitable accreditation—measures of success which AFM can directly impact. No matter the bar—be it higher SAT scores, higher graduation rates, lower transfer or attrition numbers, better job placement, or other means of measurement—AFM offers a simple and effective means to demonstrate improvement in all elements of the academic experience and environment.

CHAPTER SIX

THE PRACTICE OF
EFFECTIVE PRACTICE

Tourist in New York to a passerby: 'How do you get to Carnegie Hall?'
The local's answer: 'Practice, practice, practice.'

That particular joke may have whiskers on it, but it illustrates a powerful truth: If you wish to accomplish anything, you need to practice.

And, to take that thought a step further, to make progress toward any meaningful goal, you need to practice effectively. That's what the Academy for MOmentum (AFM) helps all sorts of individuals and groups achieve.

That begs a devil's advocate question: Don't we all know how to practice something?

Not necessarily. That's why, within the context of understanding and leveraging the dynamic principles of the AFM methodology, it's important to embrace the value of practice.

THE HISTORY OF PRACTICE

The concept of practicing the skill of practice is by no means a recent discovery among scientists and others interested in how we as human beings learn things and get better at them. Noted German psychologist Hermann Ebbinghaus conducted extensive research in the latter part of the nineteenth century on how people best retain information. Although his actual findings are a good deal more involved, the answer can be boiled down to one simple construct: Retention of information (memory) improves as a function of the number of times the information has been studied over a period of time. In his 2008 book *Outliers: The Story of Success*, author Malcolm Gladwell has written a fascinating chapter around "the 10,000-hour rule," or true expertise. The 10,000 hours refers to the actual number of hours a person (or group) needs to practice to achieve world-class performance.

No matter what source is consulted, what is indisputable is that deliberate, focused practice over time results in improved performance. The number of practice hours for most people (yes, some people are born with innate talent requiring less practice hours) results in improved performance. The more you practice, the better you get.

Additionally, learning and developing habits through repetition comes from addressing and mastering smaller components that comprise a certain task, skill, or behavior. For example, efficient swimming—including strokes and kicks—probably has several subsets: the position of the swimmer's head, the pull of the arm through the stroke shoulder rotation, efficient breathing, position alignment, and other elements. Improve in any or all of these areas and you become a better swimmer.

In another example, a competent motorcycle rider knows that there are four fundamental steps—smaller components—to every smooth and successful turn (the process) while riding. When making a turn, he or she must slow (reduce speed), look (turn your head and look as far as possible through the turn), roll (gradually roll on the throttle), and press (place forward pressure on the appropriate handgrip using the technique of counter-steering). This process is commonly referred to as SLRP (slow, look, roll, and press) and each step can be practiced individually as well as collectively.

Subcomponents, or steps, can also be added to an existing pro-cess when necessary. Consider the habit of brushing your teeth to maintain good oral hygiene. Most of us complete the steps of brushing and rinsing on a regular basis—that's rote activity. One way to improve overall oral care is daily flossing (I would suspect that most of us have heard that advice from our dental profes-sionals on more than one occasion). That step of flossing the cor-rect way, in the right sequence, daily, over a long period of time until a habit is formed, is an example of leveraging the power of deliberate practice. There are many other similar examples, from drinking more water daily to positive behavior during family ac-tivities to following through on advice from a counselor, coach, clergy, therapist, or healthcare professional.

Those varied elements also point out an essential issue that many of us might tend to overlook with regard to practice: We take it for granted. Not only does that mean that we can often downplay its value in acquiring and mastering new skills, but that we oversimplify our attitude and approach to practice. Put another way: What's the big deal about practice? You just do something over and over until you get better at it.

Nothing could really be farther from the truth, particularly with regard to the AFM program. To gain an increasing level of skill and accomplishment at anything, it's important to know exactly how you're going to practice and why you're doing it in that fashion. Or, as I often ask people who say they want to practice a skill to improve: "That's great. Describe your practice plan." A typical response outlines the *why* and *what* of the desired improvement but rarely defines the *how*.

REPETITION IS NOT PRACTICE

AFM allows users to improve their skills through a thoughtful, deliberate, focused regimen of practice with increasing levels of challenge and complexity. The success of the program illustrates the important point that repetition—simply doing something over and over without giving any real thought to it—simply isn't deliberate practice.

One overriding reason for that is that any skill, no matter how seemingly simple on the surface, involves a great deal more than first meets the eye. Similar to the examination of the action of swimming, throwing a ball may seem a straightforward enough task but, broken down, it involves the torque of the shoulder and elbow, the eyes focusing on the target, the grip on the ball, leg movement and placement, and other parts integrated to move the ball accurately across a distance.

That complexity is why AFM is so effective in teaching users the value of the practice of practicing. Since the system allows you to choose whatever particular part of a skill or behavior you wish to master—say, in throwing a ball, and working to improve your aim—your focus is fixed on working on that particular part of the overall task. Moreover, given that AFM allows users to closely track and measure progress, you know that you are, in fact, getting better at throwing the ball where you want it to go.

The value of integrated effort also comes into play as well. Even though you may be focused on trying to improve your aim when you throw the ball, implicitly you will improve in other areas, such as how you hold the ball and the smoothness of the overall motion when you throw it. You will become more coordinated overall. In other cases, integrated effort may also highlight areas that warrant further work. With pitching, you may have improved your stance and your shoulder rotation, but you still aren't getting the ball over the plate as you'd like. Looked at in another manner, you know what you're good at and what needs more practice for all of the elements of the task to result in better performance.

Another factor in the practice of practicing is understanding and knowing when it's time to, in effect, step up your game—to work at a higher and more challenging level to increase your overall mastery of the skill. In the case of throwing a ball, that might mean increasing your speed, throwing the ball from a greater distance, or putting more force behind the pitch. But, however things become more demanding or involved, the practice of practicing emphasizes increasing challenge and complexity—a central point of the AFM program. The challenge of the struggle is what helps us all become better at anything we choose to do.

AFM lets users understand and control all the variables that comprise effective, valuable practice, allowing for practice at increasingly challenging, yet controlled and predictable levels, as they proceed toward peak performance. Additionally, AFM's overall "practice of practicing" formula—which generates points as users increase their skill level—effectively provides measurable, constructive feedback. You know when you're getting better at something you've committed to getting better at—the numbers are there.

To wrap up, here's a story that effectively captures the value of the AFM system and its emphasis on understanding and embracing thoughtful, controlled practice. We have a friend who enjoys playing music in his spare time—so much so that he's done it for more than 30 years. Back when he started learning, practice was largely a matter of rote—scales and pieces practiced over and over until they were mastered. In its way, it was a time-tested and valid means of practice.

The problem came when our friend tried to play along with recorded music to further master a piece. Since the music was either on a record or tape, our friend often had a very hard time keeping up with the tempo. It was a matter of "race and repeat," hoping over time to learn the notes and phrasing that would allow him to finally play along with the music.

Our friend is still committed to his practice, only now he has a powerful new ally. There are several sorts of applications and software that allow users to slow down the tempo of recorded music. If our friend finds that a particular piece of music is simply too fast at full speed for him to keep up, he simply slows down the tempo of the recording so that he can effectively learn all the notes and chords at a slower, more manageable pace. Even better, as he improves, he's able to gradually speed up the tempo until he is eventually able to play it at the speed at which it's normally performed.

Sound at all familiar? And, if that controlled, measured practice allows him to get to Carnegie Hall one day, think of how AFM can use the very same system to allow us all to, in effect, reach whatever Carnegie Halls we may aspire to.

CHAPTER SEVEN

AFM IN ACTION

An ounce of practice is generally worth more than a ton of theory.

—Ernst F. Schumacher, in *Small is Beautiful: Economics as if People Mattered*

The Academy for MOmentum (AFM) system is all about results—for individuals, businesses, schools, and other sorts of organizations. And, given the natural differences all those groups can have, so, too, can goals and priorities differ.

But, the dynamics of AFM are common across all of those groups. To illustrate that, let's have a look at one type of goal and how practice in its varied forms can help achieve that objective, no matter if it's one person using the AFM method or thousands.

INDIVIDUALS: "SEEK TO UNDERSTAND"

As individuals, we often have a habit of acting in a reactionary and sometimes judgmental manner. Rather than hearing someone else's side of the story, we frequently are much too focused on what we think and feel.

Fortunately, many of us are also aware of that often problematic tendency and work to recognize it when it crops up. However, try as we might, our efforts can leave us frustrated and repeatedly locked in to that "me first" attitude.

Phrased another way, our response and our goal here might be summarized with the phrase, "Seek first to understand and then to be understood." It's certainly easy to say, but tough in execution.

Let's take an example that most of us can probably empathize with. You come home after a long day's work and your spouse or partner has a "surprise" in store—a $400 standing mixer, presented with an enthusiastic: "Isn't this great? Think of all the kinds of bread we'll be able to make with this!"

You agree that "bread" is the focal point of the moment, only in a more slang-related context.

"Four hundred bucks for a glorified blender?" you bellow. "Here we were just talking a few days ago about how we needed to watch our spending! What were you thinking?!"

The last sentence in that rant is by far the most pertinent, particularly from the standpoint of a very worthy objective—looking at something from someone else's perspective. And that's something that AFM can do wonders with.

Let's rewind things a bit. Long before the mixer appeared in your kitchen, and long before you even chatted with your significant other about the need to save money, you decided on a very worthwhile goal—to make an ongoing effort to give greater weight to your partner's point of view, no matter what the issue might be.

Here are a few ways you decided to practice to reach that objective:

◇ When your partner says something that takes you by surprise, rather than simply reacting to what he said, you ask that he clarify what he was talking about.

◇ You practice at repeating what your partner says to cement a clear interpretation: "If I understand what you're saying..."

◇ If your partner says something that, on the surface, is upsetting, you make a point of asking for additional information to allow her to express her viewpoint in a more complete manner.

◇ Then, rather than merely exploding, if something your partner says or does is upsetting, you practice expressing your feelings calmly and in as constructive a manner as possible.

◇ Following AFM guidelines, you log your deliberate practice, noticing that your goal of seeking to "understand first" is becoming much more natural and automatic.

OK, take two:

Your partner: "Isn't this great? Think of all the kinds of bread we'll be able to make with this!"

You: "That's quite a machine. But let's talk for a minute, okay? Given that we just talked about saving money, I'm concerned that we spent a lot of money on this."

From there you learn:

⬦ The mixer was $100 off its usual price.

⬦ Your partner was able to get an interest free, six-month payment schedule to spread out the cost.

⬦ She reminds you that you had also talked about making more homemade bread to eat healthier and to spend less money on store-bought products.

In turn, she learns:

⬦ Your feeling that you wished she had talked about the mixer before going out and buying it.

⬦ You're glad she was able to pay for the item over time.

The result:

⬦ You both decide to keep the mixer, since it does support your shared goal of eating better.

⬦ In the future, you both agree to discuss in advance any purchase greater than $100.

⬦ You spend a relaxing evening baking a healthy bread together using your new mixer, instead of continuing to stew over a $400 purchase.

COMPANIES: "LISTEN FIRST"

In his bestselling book *The Speed of Trust*, Steven Covey outlines thirteen forms of behavior that support outstanding performance in organizations of all sorts. Number eleven on the list is "Listen First."

Sound at all familiar? Let's see.

The head of sales knocks on your office door and sheepishly pokes his head in. "Got a minute, Jack?"

"Sure, Leigh," you reply, not bothering to look up from the invoices you had been reading. "What's up?"

Leigh drums his fingers on the door for a few seconds before continuing. "I hate to say this, but the McCovey deal fell through."

You yank your glasses off your head and toss them onto your desk. "For crying out loud, Leigh, what the (expletive deleted) happened?" Leigh begins to answer but you cut him off. "I warned you that we needed to stay on top of this 24/7, that McCovey could be a real pill, but you didn't do it, did you? That's right, isn't it, you just let things deteriorate until it all fell apart. A two million dollar sale, gone up in smoke."

In its own way, given the financial loss, that's a completely understandable reaction. But, with the AFM practice system in place in your company, the entire situation may have been completely avoidable.

Once again, let's take a few steps back. About six months ago, you recognized the need to improve communications across the entire spectrum of the company. Accordingly, you encouraged employees to participate in an AFM program designed to improve company communications.

For your part, you decided to practice a more proactive form of listening, including:

⬦ When an employee comes to talk with you in your office, you set aside any work or papers to make certain you give her your undivided attention.

⬦ If the employee has something to say that proves upsetting, you practice taking a deep breath to help focus your attention on what she's saying. Responding with words reflecting how she feels and what is upsetting her is one good technique.

⬦ Having heard what the employee has to say, the first thing you work to do is to clarify what you heard and calmly ask for a more complete explanation before you offer any response or feedback.

With six months of practice and progress under your belt, here's how what seemed like an inevitably explosive situation might have gone. The head of sales knocks on your office door. "Got a minute, Jack?"

"Sure, Leigh," you reply. You push the invoices you had been reading to the corner of your desk. "What's up?"

"I hate to say this, but the McCovey deal fell through."

You take a deep breath, followed by a thoughtful nod. "Well, I have to admit that I hate to hear it, too. Have a seat and walk me through everything that happened."

Leigh proceeds to lay out all the specifics of the now-failed transaction. Over the next ten minutes, you brainstorm together where certain missteps took place which contributed to the deal's collapse. You ask Leigh to take written notes so that he can be empowered to learn from the experience, rather than to walk away feeling like a failure.

Let's look at an even better rewind. Following your lead, Leigh decides to work on his own communication skills using the AFM system—in particular, he practices setting up a series of proactive, prearranged phone calls with every client to make certain that any problems that crop up during a transaction are addressed quickly and before they become potential deal busters.

Take three:

"Got a minute, Jack?

"Sure, Leigh. What's up?"

"Just wanted to let you know we're signing the finals on McCovey later this week."

"Top marks as usual, Leigh."

"Thanks. To be candid, things almost went down the drain a couple of weeks ago. I checked in with McCovey's attorney who, it turns out, had some issues with our warranties. Luckily, I put legal on it straight off and ironed it out before it all blew up in our faces."

"Good job. By the way, I'd like you to circulate a memo about your telephone check-in policy to all sales staff. We can save ourselves a ton of headaches using that company-wide."

"Already in the works, boss."

ACADEMIA: "SPEAK THE SAME LANGUAGE"

If you're a student or work in an academic setting, you're aware of some of the enormous learning opportunities that are constantly available. One such program—particularly at the high school and college levels—is the chance to collaborate with a student from another country on some sort of project.

That's certainly a wonderful chance to learn on a variety of levels, but it also presents some significant challenges. One obvious one is language—not merely with basic communication issues, but also cultural differences that are related to different languages.

Here's how that can play out. You teach upper level political science and a student of yours—Meghan—proposes to work with a student from France on a paper comparing the French and American revolutions. You're all for it, and Meghan begins corresponding with her French counterpart, Nicole.

One of the first goals is a list of seminal quotes from both wars—those memorable words and phrases that encapsulated both struggles. Meghan starts the process by emailing one of her favorites from Benjamin Franklin: "Either we all hang together or we will all hang separately."

Nicole quickly responds: "I don't understand!"

Meghan: "It's a play on words."

Nicole: "That does not help me!"

Meghan, becoming a bit frustrated: "Okay, just send over one of yours."

Nicole: "L'humanité a gagné sa bataille. Liberté dispose désormais d'un pays."

Meghan: "????"

Nicole: "It's a famous announcement by Lafayette."

Meghan: "Only if you speak French!"

Nicole: "Do not complain to me!"

At this point, the two students are wondering whether this cross-cultural experience was a good idea!

Once more, let's take a step back. Some three months prior to beginning the project, you suggest to Meghan that she begin working with the AFM system—in particular, on goals that can help her work more effectively with others, especially those who have very different backgrounds.

Meghan decides to practice ways to take other people's perspectives into account rather than offering her opinions and hoping that the other person will simply agree. You notice it in classroom discussions—where once Meghan would seek to dominate debate with students of differing opinions, she's becoming increasingly vocal in her willingness to adjust her ideas to accommodate others' viewpoints.

Her progress really comes to light in her work with Nicole.

Meghan: "So we agree to compile famous quotes from both wars?"

Nicole: "Yes. I think they're very telling."

Meghan, after a pause: "How about this? Not only do we put together a list of quotes, but we offer them both in French and English?"

Nicole: "Interesting. What would that do?"

Meghan: "We know the effect the American Revolution had on the French. I just wonder how some of the quotes we remember from both wars could be taken differently when they're spoken in a language other than the original?"

Nicole: "C'est magnifique!"

Meghan: "Ok, got one to start us off?"

Nicole: "Yes, just a moment. Here: 'Humanity has won its battle. Liberty now has a country.'"

Meghan: "Great! Who said that?"

Nicole: "Lafayette. It's interesting to hear it in English."

The resulting project is an educator's dream—not merely the exchange of knowledge but an impressive grasp and discussion of culture and context. In fact, Nicole and Meghan are honored at the end of the school year with a book prize citing their work together.

As Nicole said: "C'est magnifique!"

CHAPTER EIGHT

THE JOURNEY OF AFM

Focus on the journey, not the destination.
Joy is found not in finishing an activity but in doing it.

—Greg Anderson

An old adage cautions that you should be careful about what you ask for—you might just get it.

In the case of the Academy for MOmentum (AFM), nothing could be more true—or wonderful. As we've discussed over the course of this book, AFM is a powerful tool that can bring about positive changes in all sorts of settings, no matter who is using it or the particular circumstances.

Just as important, AFM is no one-shot quick fix. It's there for you always, for the entirety of whatever journey you may happen to be on.

That's an important attribute to bear in mind. Everything—individuals, businesses, organizations, schools—has a life cycle. Nothing remains the same. We are always changing and, when we use AFM, we're pursuing deliberate and focused practice geared toward improvement and managing those changes.

But, like the saying suggests, achieving something may not be universally positive. Even our greatest successes can put us in a position of having to face a whole new set of challenges.

Consider this example. A company looking to boost its revenue uses the AFM system to improve its sales staff presentation skills. Six months down the road, the results are in—sales have jumped five percent and the company has to hire four new salespeople to meet the demand.

Ironically, the company is also nose-to-nose with an entirely different set of issues. First, many of the newcomers are highly inexperienced. Production also has to ramp up to accommodate the new sales levels. And, as the company's product line expands as the result of increased income, so, too, do marketing and advertising campaigns need to be retooled to keep up with the changes.

If you see what we're getting at, boosting sales so dramatically through use of AFM might seem absolutely fantastic on the surface. And, it is—on the surface. What accompanies that success is a new crop of challenges that need to be addressed—otherwise, success may be very short-lived.

That's one of the inherent strengths of the AFM system. Not only does it allow participants to choose those goals they wish to pursue, as well as the form of practice used to achieve them, it's always available for use to take on new challenges and opportunities. Put another way, AFM doesn't push back against change—it embraces it, and allows users to do so as well.

ACADEMY FOR MOMENTUM:
BUSINESS & ACADEMIC INSTITUTION LIFE CYCLE

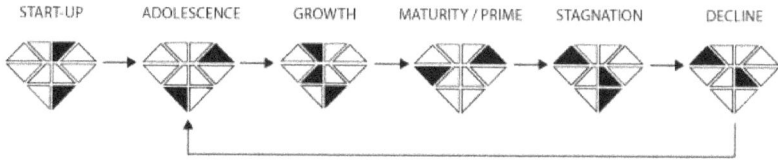

START-UP   ADOLESCENCE   GROWTH   MATURITY / PRIME   STAGNATION   DECLINE

Let's look again at our successful sales company. Lacking AFM, their recent growth might implode over time as the company is unable to adapt to changing realities. Happily, AFM doesn't allow that to happen. Using varied AFM forms of deliberate practice, newly-hired sales personnel are efficiently brought up to speed. With improved collaborative skills, the production force is empowered to boost product output. And, thanks to a balanced and thoughtful approach derived through the AFM system, marketing is better able to roll out new advertising to herald fresh, exciting products.

Consider other examples of how AFM lets users embrace the ongoing nature of change:

⬦ A mom using the AFM tool to adjust her role with her spouse and children encounters some pushback. The family members are used to Mom acting a certain way, and that has now changed. Maybe Mom has decided that she'd like her family to make their own lunches or bring their laundry down or take on more household cleaning chores. In short, Mom is scaling back on her duties to carve out more personal time for herself, as well as to encourage more responsibility in her children. She can adjust her AFM goals to help her accommodate her family's responses to her changes.

✧ A school uses AFM and effectively boosts its academic quality, attracting a higher number of applicants. That creates a new set of challenges in managing their larger applicant pool. AFM lets admission staff practice collaborative teamwork to devise better, more efficient applicant management and communication systems.

✧ A hospital makes use of AFM to improve the verbal "hand-off" of patient-related information from one unit to another. They are also able to more effectively communicate vital aftercare information to patients upon discharge, thereby improving medication and care compliance. The first outcome leads to better clinical care during the hospital stay. The second outcome, the better informed and empowered a patient is (a hospital or insurance company can provide the AFM tool to their patients), the greater the likelihood to avoid a potential readmission (through patient compliance and changing health behaviors).

These and other like examples most certainly don't end there. Unlike other solutions and systems, which can be here today, help with one problem, and gone the next, AFM inherently recognizes the dynamics of change and the ongoing need to address new issues and leverage fresh opportunities.

With improvement comes change, and, with it, a new array of challenges and issues, and so on. It's a journey with no end point.

AFM allows you to make the most of every opportunity, along every step of that journey.

I hear and I forget.
I see and I remember.
I do and I understand.

—Confucius

APPENDIX ONE

REV UP YOUR MO QUESTIONS

The Academy for MOmentum (AFM) is all about change in individuals and groups. As we discussed in this book, change can begin with any number of decisions—powerful choices that identify goals, dreams, and other issues that we'd like to pursue and, ultimately, achieve. AFM is the tool that puts all that within everyone's reach.

Sometimes, change begins with a comment or observation that takes the form of a warning, or even self-criticism: "The doctor says I need to lose twenty pounds or my health might suffer." "The boss told me I'd better learn this new software operating system quickly. I wish I could pick up on these things faster." Those aren't necessarily exclusively negative; sometimes, the most powerful and enduring force for change can come from a warning or a form of self-evaluation that pinpoints something about ourselves that we'd like to change for the better.

But change can also derive from other perspectives—a sense of opportunity, a pleasant daydream, or a sense of wanting to achieve something, not necessarily fix something.

To get the most out of the AFM system, it can be helpful to become acquainted with all sorts of questions that can kick-start all sorts of change. Since that's something that may be new to many of us, here's a sampler of questions—geared to individuals, organizations, and academic institutions—that can give you an idea of the possibilities and potential that can derive from asking the right kind of questions. Take these as guideposts and look forward to coming up with your own set of powerful questions. Spark your MO!

QUESTIONS FOR REFLECTION – INDIVIDUAL:

◇ Think back to a great book you read, one which provided many helpful tips, suggestions, or advice that really got you excited. Which of those ideas could you put to work in your own life?

◇ Have you attempted significant change in your life before? Do you know what was successful and why it was successful? Could that be applied to other areas in your life?

◇ When you attempted to change something in your life but it didn't work out, do you know why? If so, is it something you'd like to try again but with a different strategy?

◇ Can you look at goals in a new way, with a new approach? How would that approach be different?

◇ What are your current concerns? What would you like to see different in your life?

◇ Is there something you have always wanted to do that, for whatever reason, you have been unable to? Would a different approach prove more successful?

◇ Would you like to revisit old goals or consider new ones?

◇ What professional skill would you like to add that you could cite to a potential employer? Would you feel confident if you could explain the *why*, the *what*, and the *how*?

◇ Is there something you've never said to friends or loved ones that you'd like to say? Are there aspects of your personal relationships you'd like to change (or even introduce for the first time)?

YOUR **SPARK** IDEAS

QUESTIONS FOR REFLECTION – BUSINESS:

✧ Have you ever found a valuable leadership or management book that you'd like to encourage others to read and follow? What would be the most effective way to achieve that? How could you best leverage the synergy that derived from a number of people reading such a valuable book?

✧ Have you ever hired an outside speaker to come to your business or service organization—like the Lions Club or Rotary International or the Optimist Club—to inspire the team members and improve morale? What steps can be taken to leverage those insights and make them into actionable and successful changes?

✧ What leadership and organizational skills are your personal strengths? Are there ways to leverage them that you have yet to identify?

✧ How would you make the most of your employees' potential so that overall business goals are met and even exceeded?

✧ What's the most effective way to orient new staff? What about your business would you want to make sure they understand? Would trans-*form*-ative learning support your organization's vision, mission, values, and strategic plan?

✧ Does your company use a simulation lab or other experiential education program to train employees? Can you maintain the ongoing method of individual or team practice after the simulation lab is completed?

✧ If you have high employee retention, what are the aspects of your business which lead to employee contentment? How can you leverage those positive factors even more? If turnover is high, do you know the most commonly-cited causes for resignation? How can you change those for the better?

✧ How can you introduce a tool or reporting mechanism that offers real-time staff practice activity? Are your employees aware of the value of such practice? Would this tool support your organizational culture?

✧ What other new programs could you introduce that would improve employees' lives and performance, such as an exercise and health program?

✧ Do you encourage employee feedback and candor? If so, what else can you do with that information to improve the entire organization by tracking themes or common areas of concern?

✧ Have you ever attended a meeting at work and your supervisor asked the group to "use a new skill or technique"— several weeks later, some employees are practicing the skill and others are not? How were some employees able to embrace the change while others were not? What were the missing elements?

✧ Do you have a purposeful work culture that can be articulated by the staff, customers, board members, or community? Is your culture left to chance?

✧ Are the educational and/or organizational development staff and resources limited in your organization? Have you considered how to reach your staff who are located across a geographic region or who work evening or night schedules? How could the AFM tool and methodology serve these needs in a proactive and deliberate way?

⬧ What if the word "accountability" in your organization was associated with positive individual and team contributors—and the source of that accountability was the standard use of the AFM tool and methodology driving the *why*, the *what*, and the *how* in all that you do?

YOUR **SPARK** IDEAS

QUESTIONS FOR REFLECTION – ACADEMIC INSTITUTION:

◇ Do you have a system in place so you obtain feedback about what students value most about your institution? Do you have a similar system for faculty, staff, and community? How can you further leverage those positive aspects?

◇ What aspects of student life and academic performance would you like to improve? Are there measurable/definable themes that measure student life or academic performance?

◇ What aspects of faculty and staff engagement and performance would you like to improve? Has an accreditation body ever suggested the need to measure improvement to your metrics of academic success?

◇ Do you have a system in place so you know what alumni value most about your institution? How could you best use that information?

◇ Do you know what prospective students find most appealing about your institution? Is there a way to leverage that appeal? What do they find the least appealing and how may that be addressed?

◇ Do you know what prospective faculty and staff find most appealing about your institution? Is there a way to further leverage that appeal? What do they find the least appealing and how may that be addressed?

✧ Have you tried unsuccessfully in the past to change certain aspects, programs, or features of your institution? Would a different approach offer a greater chance for success?

✧ Can staff, faculty, and students articulate your school's culture? If not, why not? Is it difficult to understand or lacking in clear definition?

✧ What program—academic or otherwise—does your institution not offer now but you think would be of enormous value? What steps could you take to promote consideration and ultimate acceptance of such a program?

✧ How can you introduce a tool or reporting mechanism that offers real-time faculty, staff, and student deliberate practice activity? Do you know if they are aware of the value of such practice? Would the AFM tool provide a market differentiator for your institution?

✧ What aspects of your overall program offer students the most practical and useful value? Are there elements and programs you would like to add to bolster that practical value?

YOUR **SPARK** IDEAS

REFERENCES

1. Covey, Stephen M.R. *The SPEED of Trust: The One Thing that Changes Everything*. New York: Free Press, 2008.

2. Ebbinghaus, Hermann. *Memory: A Contribution to Experimental Psychology*. Berlin: University of Berlin, 1885.

3. Gladwell, Malcolm. *Outliers: The Story of Success*. New York: Back Bay Books, 2008. (35)

4. Mezirow, Jack & Associates. *Learning as Transformation: Critical Perspectives on a Theory in Progress*. New York: John Wiley & Sons, Inc., 2000. (21, 48, 49)

ACKNOWLEDGMENTS

If you are like me, it is truthful to say that the one person we talk with the most every day is ourselves. By that I mean we are thinkers, constantly thinking about who we are, what we are doing, our purpose, and how we relate to the many people around us. I personally have been on a path, a path that has unfolded over time, that has led me to offer insight into not only the *why* and *what* we do as individuals and groups, but also the *how*. To get to this point, I have shared my thoughts (successes, struggles, and breakthroughs) with the best team I am part of—my family. I want to acknowledge my wife Kim for her role-modeling and unwavering support; our two outstanding daughters, Jessie and Felicity; and our granddaughter Savannah. For Jessie, lending an ear (or a text message) during the writing of the book, and Felicity for providing her talents in the development of graphs and graphic art, and as a sounding board. To our beautiful granddaughter Savannah, always two steps ahead of us with her thinking and doing! To my parents, MaryAnn and James, who worked tirelessly while raising four children and role-modeling a strong work ethic.

SPARK YOUR MO

To Jerry for his bright business mind, Wayne for his creative mind, and Jeff for his insightful mind—all instrumental in getting my book off the ground. Thanks to proofreader Marcia Layton Turner for hunting down all the typos and missing commas .

I have also been blessed in my career to have been around bright, talented, and passionate people from all walks of life, accomplishing the daily miracles that make our world go 'round. It is with this gratitude that I say "thank you" and appreciate the inspiration that generated the spark to answer the question I always asked: "Now what?" For me, that is finally answered, in one way, with the creation of the Academy for MOmentum and the principles surrounding performance, transformation, and a focus on deliberate practice.

Thanks to Aloha Publishing for all their work to produce this book, including Maryanna Young for project coordination and editorial lead Jennifer Regner, and also the Fusion Creative Works design team of Shiloh Schroeder, Rachel Langaker, and Jessie Carpenter.

ABOUT THE AUTHOR

Jim Angle is the founder and CEO of Practice Field Coach LLC and the Academy for MOmentum. He has been in the healthcare field for more than 25 years, leading hospitals and high performing teams, contributing to transformational change in people and organizations, and teaching and coaching many leaders. He has a talent for "systems thinking and taking action" and a passion for not only learning, but learning through doing in a deliberate and purposeful way.

Jim has a bachelor's degree in sociology, master's degrees in social work and health systems administration, and is currently a fellow in the American College of Healthcare Executives.

Additionally, he has been an adjunct teacher for New School University and Ithaca College, and is an educational and motivational speaker, a contributor and leader on community and business boards (most recently chairman of the Idaho Hospital Association), and an endurance athlete.

Jim focuses his efforts on his endeavors with the Academy for MOmentum and Practice Field Coach LLC, from his base in New Jersey. He is married with two daughters.

ACADEMY FOR MOMENTUM

ACADEMYFORMOMENTUM.COM

1-844 MYSPARK (1-844-697-7275)

**TO EMAIL JIM, SEND TO
PFCOACHLLC@GMAIL.COM**

ABOUT THE AUTHOR

2.4 miles of swimming

112 miles of biking through mountains

26.2 miles of running

All in one day. Deliberate practice, the power of integrated effort, and MOmentum got me through.

Ironman Lake Placid, 2002

ACADEMY FOR MOMENTUM
Resources

Please visit academyformomentum.com for contact information and a current listing of services and programs offered by the Academy for MOmentum. Services include:

◇ Web-based AFM service for individuals, businesses, and academic institutions. The AFM service is purchased as a subscription (monthly fee). Individuals can sign up and activate the AFM service online at any time by following the steps and using an approved form of payment. Businesses and academic institutions: please call the AFM team to discuss your needs and aspirations, the size of your workforce and/or student body, and the partnership strategy that will accelerate your transformation.

◇ Web-based AFM service for businesses and academic institutions have the added benefit of "white labeling" the AFM service to meet their own identity, culture, and business needs. The white labeling option includes leasing the AFM program while using your own organizational name, facet descriptors, and value-based reports. Please give us a call or contact us via email to discuss this option further.

◇ Speakers: Full or partial-day speaking engagements/ workshops are available to any business, academic institution, or group. Presentations are customized to each organization's needs and time frames. Most presentations include the core AFM transformational formula and its related principles, the science behind the success, the practice of practicing, the three mastery levels, the speed of momentum, and a hands-on, practice demonstration of the offered web-based AFM service.

NOTES

www.ingramcontent.com/pod-product-compliance
Lightning Source LLC
Chambersburg PA
CBHW020157200326
41521CB00006B/405